easy
crocheted
accessories

easy
crocheted
accessories

30+ fun and
fashionable
projects

Carol Meldrum

krause publications

An F&W Publications Company

A QUARTO BOOK

Published in North America in 2006
by Krause Publications
700 East State Street
Iola, WI 54990-0001

Library of Congress Catalog Card
Number 2005935074
ISBN 0-89689-275-1

Conceived, designed, and produced by
Quarto Publishing plc
The Old Brewery
6 Blundell Street
London N7 9BH

QUA: ECA

Editor: Michelle Pickering
Art editor: Anna Knight
Designer: Jill Mumford
Photographer: Sian Irvine
Pattern checkers: Pauline Hornsby,
Hazel Williams
Assistant art director: Penny Cobb

Art director: Moira Clinch
Publisher: Paul Carslake

Color separation by
Provision Pte Ltd, Singapore
Printed by Star Standard
Pte Ltd, Singapore

materials, tools & techniques

introduction

Just like knitting, crochet is making a comeback, and has been steadily creeping into the world of fashion over the last few seasons. Crochet is now being used to make all sorts of accessories, from traditional throws and wraps to contemporary bags and jewelry items.

As a craft, the potential of crochet is almost limitless—it's quick, fun, portable, and therapeutic. With only the most basic of stitches and tools, even novice stitchers can create fabulous must-haves both to wear and to adorn the home.

The crochet hook gives you the freedom to produce all sorts of different fabrics, from open, delicate cobweb laces to chunky, compact fabrics for everyday use. Simply by changing the size of the hook or the type of yarn used, you can dramatically alter a fabric's look.

In this book, you will discover just how versatile a craft crochet is. Each technique is fully explained and illustrated in chapter 1, providing you with everything you need to know to get started. All of the projects are written in the form of easy-to-follow patterns, with step-by-step instructions on any new skills required to complete a particular item, and clear photographs of what the finished piece should look like.

The projects cover a wide spectrum of accessories, from bags and throws to hats and scarves, and include both traditional and contemporary designs. Everybody will be able to find something to suit their tastes, plus all of the projects are easily adaptable to keep up with today's fashion trends through inspired use of yarn and color. So, pick up your hook and start stitching—once you learn how to crochet, you simply won't be able to stop.

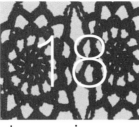

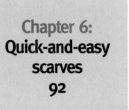

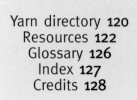

contents

Chapter 1: Materials, tools & techniques 10

Quick-and-easy projects

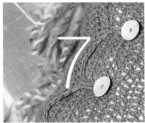
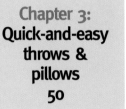
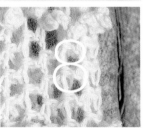

IN THIS CHAPTER YOU WILL FIND EVERYTHING YOU NEED TO KNOW ABOUT

STARTING TO CROCHET, INCLUDING INFORMATION ABOUT DIFFERENT FIBERS,

YARNS, HOOKS, AND OTHER TOOLS, AND CLEAR STEP-BY-STEP INSTRUCTIONS

ON HOW TO WORK THE BASIC STITCHES AND TECHNIQUES. THESE SKILLS

PROVIDE THE BASIS OF ALL FORMS OF CROCHET, AND ONCE YOU HAVE

LEARNED THEM, YOU WILL BE EQUIPPED TO TACKLE YOUR FIRST PROJECT.

Materials

You can create a crochet fabric from almost any continuous length of fiber, but yarn is the most commonly used material. Yarns for crochet come in a wide variety of fibers, weights, colors, and price ranges, and it is important to choose the right yarn to suit your project. Although the specific yarns used to make the projects are listed on pages 120–1, you may wish to crochet a project using a different yarn. Understanding the qualities of the various types of yarn available will help you choose one that is suitable.

Yarn

Yarns are usually made by spinning together different types of fibers. The fibers may be natural materials obtained from animals or plants, for example wool or cotton, or they can be manmade fibers such as nylon or acrylic. Yarns may be made from one fiber or combine a mixture of two or three different ones in varying proportions. Several fine strands of yarn (called "plies") are often twisted together to make thicker weights of yarn. Novelty yarns, such as tweeds and other textured yarns, combine several strands of different weights and textures twisted together.

Metallic and ribbon yarns are constructed by knitting very fine yarn into tubes and giving them a rounded or flattened appearance. As a general rule, the easiest yarns to use for crochet, especially for a beginner, have a smooth surface and a medium or tight twist.

Yarn is sold by weight, rather than by length, although the packaging of many yarns does include length per ball as well as other information. It is usually packaged into balls, although some yarns may come in the form of hanks or skeins that need to be wound by hand into balls before you can begin to crochet. The length of yarn in the ball varies from yarn to yarn, depending on thickness and fiber composition.

MOHAIR

WOOL

SILK

Animal fibers

Wool is the most commonly used natural fiber because it is soft, warm to wear, relatively inexpensive, and keeps its shape well. Woolen yarns are spun from the short fleeces of sheep. Other, more expensive animal fibers include mohair and cashmere (from goats), angora (from angora rabbits) and alpaca, and are shorn or combed from the animal before being spun into yarn. Woolen yarns (or blended yarns with a high proportion of wool) feel nice to crochet with because they have a certain amount of stretch, making it easy to push the point of the hook into each stitch. Some yarns made from pure wool have to be laundered carefully by hand, although many are now treated to make them machine washable. Silk, spun from the unwound cocoons of the silkworm, is also a natural product. Silk yarn—like wool—is a good insulator and has a delightful luster, although it has less resilience and is much more expensive.

COTTON

Vegetable fibers

Both cotton and linen are derived from plants and are popular choices for summer garments as well as home furnishings. Crochet fabric made from cotton is durable and cool to wear, but pure cotton may lack resilience and is often blended with other fibers. Pure cotton and linen yarns are also rather prone to shrinkage. Rayon (viscose), a plant-based, manmade material, is soft and slightly shiny, and because it lacks elasticity, it is usually combined with other fibers.

Synthetic fibers

Acrylic, nylon, polyester, and other synthetic fibers are manufactured from coal and petroleum products and are often made to resemble natural fibers. Yarns made wholly from synthetic fibers are usually less expensive, and although they are stable, machine washable, and do not shrink, they can lose their shape when heat is applied. The best solution is to choose a yarn where a small or equal proportion of synthetic fibers has been combined with a natural fiber such as wool or cotton. This makes them more elastic to help keep their shape when crocheted.

Yarn weights

Yarns are available in a range of thicknesses, referred to as weights, varying from very fine to very bulky. Although each weight of yarn is described by a specific name, there may actually be a lot of variation in the thicknesses when yarns are produced by different manufacturers or in different countries.

The most commonly used weights of yarn, including those used in this book, are:

sport/4-ply
- Fine yarns that are usually crocheted on hook sizes B–E (2.5–3.5 mm).

double knitting (DK)
- Slightly less than twice the thickness of sport-weight or 4-ply yarns, usually crocheted on hook sizes E–G (3.5–4.5 mm).

worsted
- Just under twice the thickness of DK, crocheted on hook sizes H–J (5–6 mm).

aran
- Also just under twice the thickness of DK and crocheted on hook sizes H–J (5–6 mm).

bulky
- Any chunky yarn that is thicker than worsted or Aran, crocheted on hook sizes J–K (6–7 mm).

super bulky
- Really fat yarns, variously termed extra bulky, super bulky, or extra super bulky, crocheted on hook sizes L (8 mm) upward.

LINEN

VISCOSE/POLYESTER

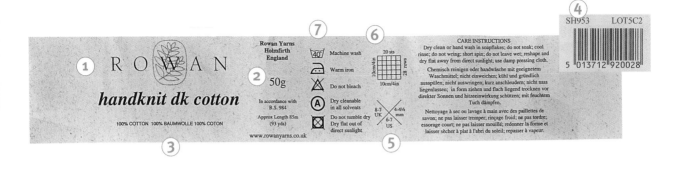

Ball bands

Whether it comes in ball or hank form, the yarn you buy will have a band around it that lists lots of important information.

1   **Company brand and yarn name.**

2   **Weight and length:** This gives the weight of the ball in ounces or grams and the length of the yarn in meters or yards. This information is useful for calculating the total length needed to complete a project. You can then compare alternative yarns to see whether more or fewer balls are needed to match the required length.

3   **Fiber content.**

4   **Shade and dye lot numbers:** The shade number is the manufacturer's reference to a particular color; the dye lot number refers to a specific batch of yarn dyed in that color at the same time. The lot number will change from batch to batch. When crocheting a project, it is important to buy sufficient yarn from the same dye lot because different dye lots can vary slightly in color. If you are not certain how many balls you will need, it is always best to buy one extra.

5   **Needle size:** This gives the generally recommended knitting needle size to use. Some brands also give the generally recommended crochet hook size to use.

6   **Gauge:** This is the standard number of stitches and rows measured over 4" (10 cm) using the recommended knitting needle size and stockinette stitch.

7   **Washing instructions:** These tell you how to wash and take care of the yarn when crocheted.

Substituting yarns

The specific yarns used to crochet the patterns in this book are listed on pages 120–1, but you can substitute an alternative yarn if you prefer or if you cannot find the exact yarn used. However, there are a number of things that you need to check before purchasing a substitute yarn.

- Calculate the total length of yarn needed to complete the project by multiplying the number of balls by the length of yarn per ball (you will find this information at the beginning of each project).

- Then divide the total length of yarn required by the length per ball of the substitute yarn. This will give the number of substitute balls required.

- Check that the substitute yarn is the equivalent weight of the yarn used to make the project.

- If felting is included in the pattern, check to see that the substituted yarn fibers are suitable—that is, not cotton, superwash wool, or synthetic, because these yarn fibers will not felt.

Yarns, such as the 100% cotton yarn used to make this bag (pages 42–3) are available in a fantastic range of colors to suit all tastes.

Beads and sequins

Beads and sequins can add a touch of glamour to a crocheted garment and are great for embellishing jewelry. When choosing beads, check whether or not they are machine washable. Also take into consideration the weight of yarn you are using. For example, do not use large glass beads on a light-weight fabric because they will cause the crochet to sag. Glass and wooden beads are used for projects in this book.

Sequins are usually made of plastic, so avoid dry cleaning, pressing, or steaming them. Round sequins can be either flat or cupped—that is, the edges are faceted and tilt up toward the central hole. Take care when using the cupped variety that they face away from the surface of the crochet or their edges can damage the yarn.

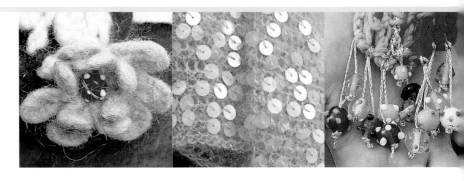

Jewelry wire

Yarn is not the only material you can crochet with. The beaded bracelet on page 112 is made from a reel of jewelry wire. Beads can be threaded directly onto the wire without using a needle even when the wire is soft and flexible enough to crochet. Thicker wires are more difficult to crochet than thinner wires.

Buttons

Buttons can make or break a project, so it is worth spending a little more for an interesting button that will enhance your crochet piece. Shell and pearlized buttons are used for the projects in this book. Always buy buttons after working the buttonholes to ensure a good fit.

Other materials

Other materials used to make the projects in this book include pillow forms, bamboo handles, a zipper, jewelry fastenings, and embroidery thread. These can all be purchased from good haberdashery stores.

Tools

POINT ——— THROAT   THUMB REST   SHANK

Very little equipment is needed for crochet—all you really need is a hook, although items such as pins and sharp scissors are useful and relatively inexpensive. The tools mentioned here are the basics; others can be bought as you go along.

Hooks

Crochet hooks are available in a wide range of sizes, shapes, and materials. The most common sorts of hooks used for working with the types of yarns covered in this book are made from aluminum or plastic. Small sizes of steel hooks are also made for working crochet with very fine cotton yarns. (This type of fine yarn is known as crochet thread.) Some brands of aluminum and steel hooks have plastic handles to give a better grip (often called "soft touch" handles) and make the work easier on the fingers. Handmade wooden and horn hooks are also available, many featuring decorative handles. Bamboo hooks are great to work with because they are made from a natural material and have a very smooth finish.

Crochet hooks come in a range of sizes, from very fine to very thick. Finer yarns usually require a smaller hook, thicker yarns a larger hook. There appears to be no standardization of hook sizing between manufacturers. The points and throats of different brands of hooks often vary in shape, which affects the size of stitch they produce.

Hook sizes are quoted differently in the United States and Europe, and some brands of hooks are labeled with more than one type of numbering. The hook sizes quoted in pattern instructions are a very useful guide, but you may find that you need to use smaller or larger hook sizes, depending on the brand, to achieve the correct gauge for the pattern (see page 31).

Choosing a hook is largely a matter of personal preference and will depend on various factors such as hand size, finger length, weight of hook, and whether you like the feel of aluminum or plastic in your hand. The most important things to consider when choosing a hook is how it feels in your hand and the ease with which it works with your yarn. When you have found your perfect brand of hook, it is useful to buy a range of several different sizes. Store your hooks in a clean container—you can buy a fabric roll with loops to secure the hooks, or use a zippered pouch such as a cosmetic bag.

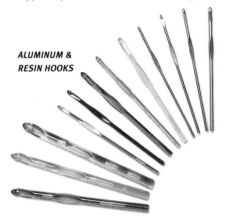

ALUMINUM & RESIN HOOKS

Comparative crochet hook sizes (from smallest to largest)

Steel			Aluminum or Plastic		
US	UK	METRIC (MM)	US	UK	METRIC (MM)
14	6	0.60		14	2.00
13	5½			13	
12	5	0.75	B	12	2.50
11	4½		C	11	3.00
10	4	1.00	D	10	
9	3½		E	9	3.50
8	3	1.25	F	8	4.00
7	2½	1.50	G	7	4.50
6	2	1.75	H	6	5.00
5	1½		I	5	5.50
4	1	2.00	J	4	6.00
3	1/0		K	2	7.00
2	2/0	2.50	L	1	8.00
1	3/0	3.00	N	0	9.00
0			P	00	10.00
00		3.50			

MARKERS

GLASS-HEADED PINS

ROW COUNTER

QUILTERS' PINS

Markers

Split rings or shaped loops made from brightly colored plastic can be slipped onto your crochet to mark a place on a pattern, to indicate the beginning row of a repeat, and to help with counting the stitches on the foundation chain.

Sewing needles

Tapestry needles have blunt points and long eyes and are normally used for counted thread embroidery. They come in a range of sizes and are used for weaving in yarn ends and for sewing pieces of crochet together. Very large blunt-pointed needles are often labeled as "yarn needles." You may also need a selection of sewing needles with sharp points for applying crochet edging, working embroidery stitches, and so on.

Pins

Glass-headed rustproof pins are the best type to use for blocking (see pages 32–3). Plastic-headed or pearl-headed pins can be used for pinning crochet and for cold-water blocking, but do not use this type for warm-steam blocking because the heat of the iron will melt the plastic heads. Quilters' long pins with fancy heads are useful when pinning pieces of crochet together because the heads are easy to see and will not slip through the crochet fabric.

Tape measure

Choose one that shows both inches and centimeters on the same side and replace it when it becomes worn or frayed because this means it will probably have stretched and become inaccurate. A 12" (30 cm) metal or plastic ruler is also useful for measuring gauge swatches.

Row counter

A knitter's row counter will help you keep track of the number of rows you have worked, or you may prefer to use a notebook and pencil.

Sharp scissors

Choose a small, pointed pair to cut yarn and trim off yarn ends.

Notebook

Keep a small notebook handy to record where you are in the pattern or any changes you have made.

SEWING NEEDLES

TAPE MEASURE

SHARP SCISSORS

Getting started

The first step when beginning to crochet is to create a foundation chain of loops. It is also important to hold the hook and yarn correctly. There are numerous ways of doing this, but the best method is the one that feels most comfortable to you.

Holding the hook

There are a few different methods of holding the hook and yarn. There is no right or wrong way. The most important thing is to use the method that you prefer and the type of hook that you find most comfortable.

Holding the yarn

It is important to wrap the yarn around your fingers to control the supply of yarn and to keep the gauge even. You can hold the yarn in several ways, but again it is best to use the method that feels the most comfortable.

Pen hold

Hold the hook as if it were a pen, with the tips of your thumb and forefinger over the flat section or middle of the hook.

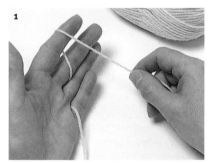

1 Loop the short end of the yarn over your forefinger, with the yarn coming from the ball under the next finger. Grip the length of yarn coming from the ball gently with your third and little fingers.

Knife hold

Hold the hook as if it were a knife, almost grasping the flat section or middle of the hook between your thumb and forefinger.

2 Alternatively, loop the short end of the yarn over your forefinger, with the yarn coming from the ball under your next two fingers and then wrapped around the little finger.

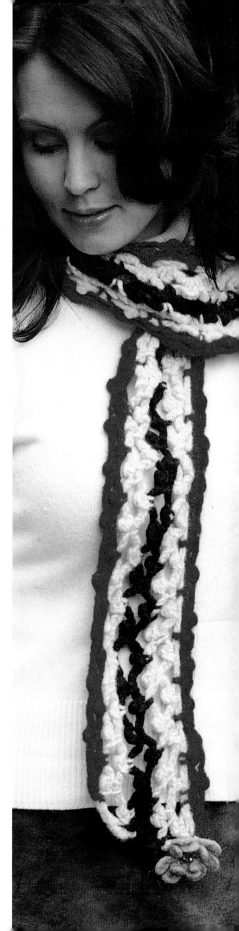

Like all crochet, this scarf (pages 102–3) begins with a simple slip knot and a foundation chain of stitches.

Making a slip knot

All crochet is made up from one loop on the hook at any time. The first working loop begins as a slip knot. The first loop does not count as a stitch.

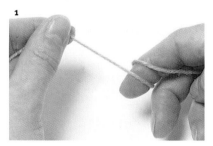

1 Take the short end of the yarn in one hand and wrap it around the forefinger on your other hand.

2 Slip the loop off your forefinger and push a loop of the short end of the yarn through the loop from your forefinger.

3 Insert the hook into this second loop. Gently pull the short end of the yarn to tighten the loop around the hook and complete the slip knot.

Foundation chains

From the slip knot, you can now create a foundation chain (this is similar to casting on in knitting). This chain determines the width of the work.

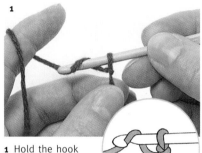

1 Hold the hook with the slip knot in one hand. With your other hand, grip the shorter piece of yarn just under the slip knot with your thumb and middle finger, and hold the longer piece of yarn over the forefinger. To create the first chain stitch, use your forefinger to wrap the yarn over the hook (known as "yarn over").

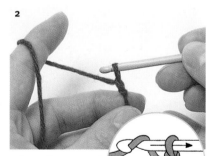

2 Draw the wrapped yarn toward you and through the slip knot already on the hook to make a new loop and complete the chain stitch.

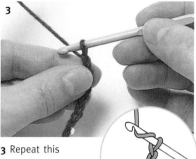

3 Repeat this process, remembering to move your thumb and middle finger up the chain as it lengthens. When counting the chain stitches, each V-shaped loop on the front of the chain counts as one, except the one on the hook, which is known as a working stitch.

TIP: COUNTING STITCHES

The front of the chain looks like a series of V shapes, while the back of the chain forms a distinctive "bump" of yarn behind each V shape. When counting chain stitches, count each V shape on the front of the chain as one chain stitch, except for the chain stitch on the hook, which is not counted. You may find it easier to turn the chain over and count the "bumps" on the back of the chain.

Working into the foundation chain

The first row of stitches is worked into the foundation chain. There are two ways of doing this, with the first method being easiest for the beginner.

1 Hold the chain with the front (V shapes) facing you. Insert the hook into the top loop of each chain stitch. This gives a loose edge to a piece of crochet.

2 Hold the chain with the back ("bumps") facing you. Insert the hook into the "bump" at the back of each chain stitch. This makes a stronger, neater edge.

Turning chains

When working crochet either in rows or rounds, you need to work a specific number of extra chain stitches at the beginning of a row or round. These stitches are called a turning chain when worked at the beginning of a straight row and a starting chain when worked at the beginning of a round. What they do is bring the hook up to the correct height for the next stitch to be worked, so the longer the stitch, the longer the turning chain that is necessary.

The patterns in this book specify how many chain stitches need to be worked at the beginning of a row or round. The list below shows the standard number of chain stitches needed to make a turn for each type of basic crochet stitch, but a pattern may vary from this in order to produce a specific effect. If you have a tendency to work chain stitches very tightly, you may need to work an extra chain stitch in order to keep the edges of your work from becoming too tight.

Number of turning chain stitches

- Single crochet = 1 turning chain
- Extended single crochet = 2 turning chains
- Half double crochet = 2 turning chains
- Double crochet = 3 turning chains
- Treble crochet = 4 turning chains

TIP: WORKING WITH TURNING CHAINS

The turning or starting chain is counted as the first stitch of the row except when working single crochet, when the turning chain is ignored. At the end of the row or round, the final stitch is usually worked into the turning or starting chain of the previous row or round.

Longer stitches, such as the treble crochet used to make this shrug (pages 84–5), require more turning chains than short stitches such as single crochet.

Basic stitches

Various stitches can be worked onto the foundation chain to form a crochet fabric. Each stitch gives a different texture and varies in depth.

TIP: NUMBER OF CHAINS

This diagram shows the number of chains from the hook. Different crochet stitches are worked a different number of chains from the hook. For example, single crochet is usually worked through the second chain from the hook, while double crochet is worked through the fourth chain from the hook.

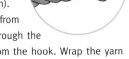

Single crochet (sc)

This is the easiest of crochet fabrics to create, producing a compact fabric that is still flexible.

1 Work the foundation chain plus one extra chain stitch (this is the turning chain). Insert the hook from front to back through the second chain from the hook. Wrap the yarn over the hook and draw the yarn through the chain toward you, leaving two loops on the hook.

3 Continue in this way along the row, working one single crochet stitch into each chain stitch.

4 At the end of the row, turn and work one chain for the turning chain. When working single crochet back along the row, insert the hook from front to back under both loops of the single crochet stitches of the previous row.

5 Fabric composed entirely of single crochet stitches is compact but flexible.

Slip stitch (sl st)

This is commonly used to join ends of work together to form a ring or to work across the top of other stitches invisibly. Insert the hook from front to back into the last chain just worked. Wrap the yarn over the hook, then draw the yarn toward you through both the chain and the loop on the hook.

2 Wrap the yarn over the hook again and draw it through both loops on the hook. This leaves one loop on the hook and completes the stitch.

Extended single crochet (exsc)

As its name suggests, this stitch is slightly longer than a single crochet stitch.

1 Work the foundation chain plus two extra chain stitches (this is the turning chain). Insert the hook from front to back through the third chain from the hook. Wrap the yarn over the hook and draw the yarn through the chain toward you, leaving two loops on the hook.

2 Wrap the yarn over the hook again and draw it through the first loop on the hook, again leaving two loops on the hook.

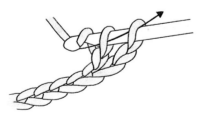

3 Wrap the yarn over the hook again and draw it through both loops on the hook.

4 This leaves one loop on the hook and completes the stitch. Continue in this way along the row, working one extended single crochet into each chain stitch. At the end of the row, turn and work two chains for the turning chain. When working extended single crochet back along the row, insert the hook from front to back under both loops of the extended single crochet stitches of the previous row.

Double crochet (dc)

Double crochet is a longer stitch than single crochet, creating a more open and flexible fabric. The stitch is worked in a similar way to single crochet, except that you wrap the yarn over the hook before working into the fabric.

1 Work the foundation chain plus three extra chain stitches (this is the turning chain). Wrap the yarn over the hook, then insert the hook from front to back into the fourth chain from the hook.

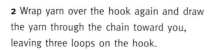

2 Wrap yarn over the hook again and draw the yarn through the chain toward you, leaving three loops on the hook.

3 Wrap the yarn over the hook again and draw it through the first two loops, leaving two loops on the hook.

4 Wrap the yarn over the hook again and draw it through the last two loops.

5 This leaves one loop on the hook and completes the stitch. Continue in this way along the row, working one double crochet into each chain stitch.

6

6 At the end of the row, turn and work three chains for the turning chain. When working double crochet back along the row, skip the first double crochet stitch at the beginning of the row and insert the hook from front to back though both loops of each remaining double crochet stitch of the previous row. At the end of the row, work the last stitch into the top of the turning chain.

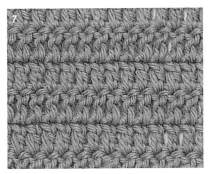

7 Fabric composed entirely of double crochet stitches is still firm, like single crochet fabric, but slightly more open and flexible.

Half double crochet (hdc)

This stitch is slightly shorter than the double crochet stitch.

1

1 Work the foundation chain plus two extra chain stitches (this is the turning chain). Wrap the yarn over the hook, then insert the hook from front to back into the third chain from the hook.

2

2 Wrap yarn over the hook again and draw the yarn through the chain toward you, leaving three loops on the hook. Wrap the yarn over the hook again and draw it through all three loops. This leaves one loop on the hook and completes the stitch.

3

3 Continue in this way along the row, working one half double crochet into each chain stitch. At the end of the row, turn and work two chains for the turning chain.

4

4 When working half double crochet back along the row, skip the first half double crochet stitch at the beginning of the row, then insert the hook from front to back under both loops of each remaining half double crochet stitch of the previous row.

5

5 At the end of the row, work the last stitch into the top of the turning chain.

6

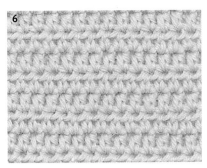

6 Fabric composed entirely of half double crochet stitches is firm and flexible, but not as compact as single crochet or double crochet fabric.

Treble crochet (tr)

This stitch is slightly longer than double crochet stitch.

1 Work the foundation chain plus four extra chain stitches (this is the turning chain). Wrap the yarn over the hook twice, then insert the hook from front to back into the fifth chain from the hook. Wrap the yarn over the hook again and draw the yarn through the chain toward you, leaving four loops on the hook.

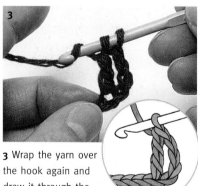

2 Wrap the yarn over the hook again and draw it through the first two loops, leaving three loops on the hook.

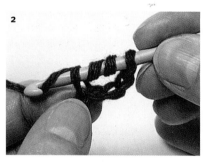

3 Wrap the yarn over the hook again and draw it through the first two loops, leaving two loops on the hook. Wrap the yarn over the hook again and draw it under the last two loops. This leaves one loop on the hook and completes the stitch.

4 Continue in this way along the row, working one treble crochet into each chain stitch. At the end of the row, turn and work four chains for the turning chain. When working treble crochet back along the row, skip the first treble crochet stitch at the beginning of the row, then insert the hook from front to back through both loops of the remaining treble crochet stitches of the previous row. At the end of the row, work the last stitch into the top of the turning chain.

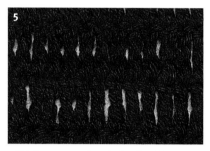

5 Fabric composed entirely of treble crochet stitches is open and very flexible.

Working into front and back of stitches

It is usual to work crochet stitches under both loops of the stitches made on the previous row. However, sometimes a pattern will instruct you to work under just one loop, either the back or the front, in which case the remaining loop becomes a horizontal bar.

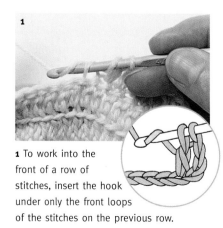

1 To work into the front of a row of stitches, insert the hook under only the front loops of the stitches on the previous row.

2 To work into the back of a row of stitches, insert the hook under only the back loops of the stitches on the previous row. Working into the back of the stitch creates a strongly ridged fabric.

Joining a new yarn or color

Whether you are joining a new ball of yarn or a new color for stripes, the method is the same. It is best to join a new yarn at the end of a row, but you can join a new yarn anywhere in a row if you need to. Leave the last stage of the final stitch incomplete, loop the new yarn around the hook, and use it to complete the stitch. Work the next row in the new yarn or color. When changing color in the middle of a row, begin the stitch in the usual way, wrap the new yarn over the hook, draw the new yarn through the stitch toward you, and then work the stitch.

Working in rounds

Some circular pieces of crochet require that you work in rounds rather than rows. The basic stitch techniques are the same, but you work around the work rather than back and forth.

Making a ring

To start, you have to make a ring by joining a small length of chain with a slip stitch. The chain is usually between 4 and 6 stitches, depending on the thickness of yarn being used.

3

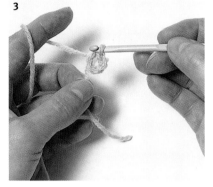

3 Gently tighten the first stitch by pulling the loose yarn end. You have now created a ring of chains.

Working into the ring

The foundation ring is the center of your circular crochet and where you will work into on the next round.

1

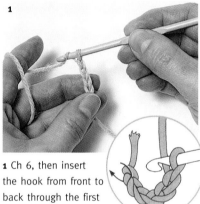

1 Ch 6, then insert the hook from front to back through the first chain made.

2

2 Wrap the yarn over the hook and draw it toward you through the chain and loop on the hook, as if working a slip stitch (see page 21).

1

1 Depending on the stitch you will be using, make the appropriate length of starting chain (see page 20).

2

2 Insert the hook from front to back into the center of the ring (not into the chain) for each stitch and work the number of stitches specified in the pattern. Remember when working in rounds that the right side is always facing you.

3

3 When you have worked around the full circle, finish off the round by working a slip stitch into the top of the starting chain worked at the beginning of the round.

TIP: MARKING ROUNDS

Place a marker at the beginning of the round. This will help to show where the round stops and starts because sometimes it can be tricky to tell. Simply pull the marker out at the end of each round and reposition it for the next.

Shaping techniques

Shaping your crochet is done by increasing or decreasing stitches along a row. When adding or subtracting stitches at intervals along a row, this is called internal increase or decrease. When stitches are added or subtracted at the beginning or end of a row, this is called external increase or decrease. Each method creates a different effect.

2 On the next row, work the extra stitches along the chain and then continue along the row.

Internal increases

This is the simplest method of adding stitches at intervals along a row.

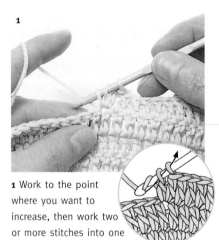

1 Work to the point where you want to increase, then work two or more stitches into one stitch on the previous row.

3 At the end of the row, work to the last two stitches, work the increase in the next to last stitch as described in step 1, and then work the last stitch.

External increases

This method can be used to increase several stitches at one time. You will need to add extra foundation chains at the beginning or end of a row.

3 To add stitches at the end of a row, leave the last few stitches of the row unworked. Remove the hook and join a length of yarn to the last stitch of the row and work the required number of extra foundation chains. Fasten off the yarn.

2 This method is often used one stitch in from the edge at the beginning and end of a row to shape garment edges neatly. At the beginning of the row, work the first stitch and then work the increase as described in step 1.

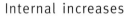

1 To add stitches at the beginning of a row, work the required number of extra chains at the end of the previous row and remember to add the turning chains.

4 Place the hook back into the row, complete the row, and then continue working extra stitches across the chain.

Internal decreases

As with the internal increases, if you are decreasing stitches in order to create a neat edge when shaping, always work the decrease one stitch in from the edge.

1 The easiest way to decrease stitches across a row is simply to skip one stitch of the previous row.

2 Alternatively, two stitches can be worked together. Start working the first stitch of the decrease but do not complete it; instead, leave two loops on the hook. Insert the hook into the next stitch and work another incomplete stitch so that you have three loops on the hook. Wrap the yarn over the hook and draw it through all three loops on the hook.

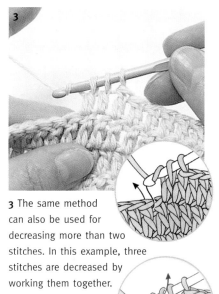

3 The same method can also be used for decreasing more than two stitches. In this example, three stitches are decreased by working them together.

External decreases

This method is best used if you want to decrease several stitches at one time.

1 To decrease at the beginning of a row, work a slip stitch (see page 21) into each of the stitches that you want to decrease, then work the turning chains and continue along the row.

2 To decrease at the end of a row, leave the stitches to be decreased unworked. Work the turning chains, then turn and work along the next row.

Shaping techniques, used to make projects such as this lacy cape (pages 78–9), are easy to learn.

Lace work

Lace motifs are light, pretty, and delicate to look at when worked in light-weight yarns, and are perfect for making shawls, wraps, and stoles. It is usual to join several motifs to make a strip, then add further motifs along one long edge of the strip until you have two strips joined together. Keep adding motifs until you have joined the required number of strips together.

Chain spaces

Long strands of chain stitches, described as chain spaces, chain loops, or chain arches, are an integral part of lace motif patterns. They are sometimes used as a foundation for stitches worked in the following round, or they may form a visible part of the design.

Changing the hook position

of a petal in order to move the hook and yarn from the valley between two petals to the tip of one petal, ready to work the next sequence of stitches.

Working in slip stitch (see page 21) across one or more stitches is a useful way of changing the position of the yarn and hook on a round. Pattern directions may refer to this technique as "slip stitch across" or "slip stitch into." Here, slip stitches are being worked into the edge

Lace motifs are very effective when joined together to make garments such as the lace evening wrap (pages 82–3).

1 Work chain spaces as evenly as possible, anchoring them by working a slip stitch or single crochet into the previous round.

2 When a chain space is worked as a foundation on one row, stitches are worked over the chains on the following row. To do this, simply insert the hook into the space below the strand of chain stitches to work each stitch, not directly into individual chain stitches.

Joining lace motifs

Lace motifs are usually joined together on the final pattern round as you work, eliminating the need for sewing.

1 Complete the first motif. Work the second motif up to the last round, then work the first side of the last round, ending at the specified point where the first join will be made, in this case halfway along a chain space at the corner of the motif.

2 Place the first and second motifs wrong sides together, ready to work the next side of the second motif. Join the chain spaces with a single crochet stitch, then complete the chain space on the second motif. Continue along the same side of the second motif, joining chain spaces together with single crochet stitches.

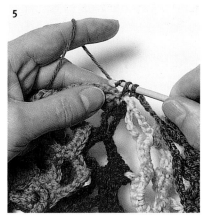

3 After all the chain spaces along one side are joined, complete the second motif in the usual way. Work additional motifs in the same way, joining the required number together to make a strip.

4 Work the first motif of the second strip, stopping when you have reached the joining point. Place against the side of the top motif in the first strip (wrong sides together) and join the chain spaces as before. When you reach the point where three corner chain spaces meet, work the single crochet into the stitch joining two existing motifs.

5 Work the second motif of the second strip, stopping when you have reached the joining point. Place against the side of the first motif in the second strip (wrong sides together) and join the chain spaces as before. When you reach the point where all four corner chain spaces meet, work the single crochet into the stitch joining the first two motifs.

6 Now join the next side of the motif to the adjacent side of the first strip, working single crochet stitches into chain spaces as before. Complete the remaining sides of the motif. Continue working in the same way until you have made and joined the required number of motifs.

Understanding patterns

Crochet pattern instructions are laid out in a logical sequence, although at first sight the terminology can look complicated. The most important thing is to check that you start off with the correct number of stitches in the foundation row or ring, and then work through the instructions row by row exactly as stated. All of the patterns in this book use written instructions rather than charts.

This pair of belts (pages 72–5) may look complex but the patterns are short and easy to follow.

Crochet abbreviations

The abbreviations used in this book are:

bch—beaded chain
bsc—beaded single crochet
C2—yo twice, draw loop through stitch just worked, (yo, draw loop through first 2 loops on hook) twice, skip 2 stitches, yo twice, draw loop through next stitch, (yo, draw loop through first 2 loops on hook) twice, yo, draw loop through remaining 3 loops on hook
ch—chain
dc—double crochet
dec—decrease
exsc—extended single crochet
hdc—half double crochet
inc—increase
mcs—mock cable stitch
sc—single crochet
sl st—slip stitch
sqsc—sequinned single crochet
st(s)—stitch(es)
tr—treble or triple crochet
yo—yarn over

Essential information

All patterns provide a list containing the size of the finished item, the materials and hook size required, the gauge of the piece, and the abbreviations used in the instructions. Although many abbreviations are standardized, such as ch for chain and st for stitch, some of them vary, so always read the abbreviations before you start crocheting.

Repeats

When following the pattern instructions, you will find that some of them appear within curved parentheses and some are marked with an asterisk. Instructions that appear within parentheses are to be repeated. For example, (1 dc into next 3 sts, ch 2) 4 times means that you work the 3 double crochet stitches and the 2 chains in the sequence stated four times in all. Asterisks (*) indicate the point to which you should return when you reach the phrase "repeat from *." They may also mark whole sets of instructions that are to be repeated. For example, "repeat from * to **" means repeat the instructions between the single and double asterisks.

You may also find asterisks used in instructions that tell you how to work any stitches remaining after the last complete repeat of a stitch sequence is worked. For example, repeat from *, ending with 1 sc into each of last 2 sts, turn, means that you have two stitches left at the end of

> **TIP: TAKE NOTES**
> Each stitch pattern worked in rows is written using a specific number of pattern rows and the sequence is repeated until the crochet is the correct length. When working a complicated stitch pattern, always make a note of exactly which row you are working.

the row after working the last repeat. In this case, work one single crochet into each of the last two stitches before turning to begin the next row.

Additional information

You may find a number enclosed in parentheses at the end of a row or round. This indicates the total number of stitches to be worked in that particular row or round. For example, (12 spaced dc) at the end of a round means that you have to work 12 double crochet stitches in the round, each one spaced by the number of chains stated in the instructions.

Gauge

The term "gauge" refers to the number of stitches and rows contained in a given width and length of crochet fabric, usually 4" (10 cm) square. You will find that everybody has their own personal gauge when working a crochet fabric. It varies from person to person, even when the same yarn and hook size are used. Crochet patterns are written using a specific gauge in mind, and if your gauge differs from the one given, the finished piece could come out either too big or too small. That is why it is important to check your gauge before starting a pattern.

Making a test swatch

Using the recommended hook size and yarn, make a crochet piece approx 6–8" (15–20 cm) square, taking into account the number of stitches and rows in the stitch pattern. Fasten off the yarn and then block the gauge sample (see pages 32–3). Some stitch patterns have the effect of reducing or expanding the crochet widthwise and others have the same effect lengthwise, so it is important that you work the gauge sample in the exact pattern you will use for the main piece.

2 Turn the fabric on its side. Using a ruler or tape measure, measure 4" (10 cm) horizontally across the rows. Insert pins exactly 4" (10 cm) apart and count the number of rows (including partial rows) between the pins.

1 Lay the sample right side up on a flat surface. Using a ruler or tape measure, measure 4" (10 cm) horizontally across a row of stitches. Insert pins exactly 4" (10 cm) apart and count the number of stitches (including partial stitches) between the pins.

3 When working a stitch pattern, the gauge may be quoted as a multiple of the pattern repeat rather than a number of stitches and rows. Work the gauge sample in pattern, but count the number of pattern repeats between the pins.

Adjusting your gauge

If the number of stitches, rows, or pattern repeats to 4" (10 cm) match the pattern, you can get started. If you have too many stitches or rows or a smaller pattern repeat to 4" (10 cm), your crochet is too tight. Work another gauge sample using a larger hook. If you have too few stitches or rows or a larger pattern repeat to 4" (10 cm), your crochet is too loose. Work another gauge sample using a smaller hook. Block and measure the new gauge sample as before. Repeat this process until your gauge matches that given in the pattern.

TIP: HOOKS AND YARNS

The hook and yarn you use may affect your gauge. Hooks from different manufacturers and those made from different materials can vary in size even though they may all be branded as the same size. Similarly, two yarns with the same description (e.g. sport or bulky) and fiber content made by different manufacturers will vary slightly in thickness. The color of yarn you choose may also affect gauge as a result of the different dyes used in manufacture. Always use the same hook and yarn for working both the gauge sample and the finished item.

Finishing techniques

A beautifully crocheted garment can easily be ruined by careless sewing up. Use a tapestry needle and a length of the yarn used to crochet the project, and select the method most suitable for the finished effect you want to achieve. Most crocheted fabrics need to be blocked before they are stitched together.

Fastening off

When your work is completed, you need to fasten off the yarn to stop it from unraveling. This is called fastening off or binding off.

1 Cut the yarn, leaving a length of about 4–6" (10–15 cm). Draw the loose end through the last loop on the hook.

2 Pull the yarn end to tighten and secure it.

Weaving in ends

After fastening off the yarn, you need to weave in all the loose ends. Thread the end through a blunt-ended needle with a large eye. Weave all the loose ends into the work, running them through the stitches nearest to the yarn end.

1 At the top edge of the work, weave the end through several stitches on the wrong side. Cut off the excess yarn.

2 At the lower edge of the work, weave the end through several stitches on the wrong side. Cut off the excess yarn.

Blocking and pressing

When all the ends are woven in and before you start sewing the pieces together, you need to block and press them to the correct size and shape. To block crochet, pin the pieces onto a padded surface. Depending on the size of the piece you want to block, a variety of things can be used—ironing board, large pillow, a board covered with one or two layers of quilter's batting, or even the floor. Cover the padded surface with a check pattern cotton fabric. This will not only help when pinning straight edges, but also will withstand the heat of an iron. When choosing how to press the crochet pieces, refer to the information given on the ball band of the yarn.

1 Pin the pieces right side downward onto a padded surface using rustless glass-headed pins (plastic may melt) inserted at right angles to the edge of the crochet. Ease the crochet piece into shape, making sure that the stitches and rows are straight. Measure to check that each pinned out piece matches the finished size stated in the pattern.

2

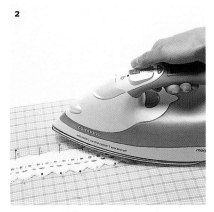

2 For natural fibers such as wool or cotton, set the iron on a steam setting. Hold the iron approximately 1" (2.5 cm) above the fabric and allow the steam to penetrate for several seconds. Work in sections and avoid the iron touching the work. Lay flat and allow to dry before removing the pins.

3

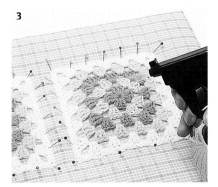

3 Pin crochet pieces made from synthetic fibers as described in step 1. Do not use a dry or a steam iron. When heat is applied to synthetics, they lose their luster and go very limp; in the worst cases you can melt the crochet and ruin your iron. When pinned out, spray the crochet fabric lightly with cold water until evenly moist but not soaked through. Lay flat and allow to dry before taking out the pins.

Seams

There are several methods for joining pieces of crochet together, including sewing the seams using a sewing needle or working a row of crochet stitches through the edges of the pieces using a crochet hook. It is really a matter of personal preference unless a pattern specifies a particular method. Use the one you are most comfortable with and that gives you the best finish. Seams are usually worked using the same yarn used for the main pieces, but a contrasting color yarn can be used to make a decorative statement. A contrasting color is used in these examples for clarity.

Overcast seam

Pieces of crochet can be joined by overcasting the seam. The overcasting stitches can be worked through just the back of the crochet loops or the whole loops. Place the pieces to be joined side by side on a flat surface with right sides facing up and edges together. Thread a large blunt-ended sewing needle with yarn.

1 Working from right to left, overcast the seam by inserting the needle into the back loop of corresponding stitches. For extra strength, you can work two stitches into the end loops.

2

2 Continue overcasting the seam, making sure you join only the back loops of the edges together, until you reach the end of the seam. Secure the yarn carefully at the beginning and end of the stitching.

3

3 Alternatively, overcast the two pieces together by inserting the needle through the whole loops of corresponding stitches. This gives a less neat join than sewing through just the back of the loops.

Backstitch seam

This creates a strong but non-elastic seam and is suitable where firmness is required and for light-weight yarns. With right sides facing each other, pin together the pieces to be joined. Insert the pins at right angles to the edge evenly across the fabric. Thread a large blunt-ended sewing needle with yarn.

1 Secure the end of the seam and yarn by taking the needle twice around the outer edges of the fabric, from back to front. Take the yarn around the outside edge once more, but this time insert the needle through the work from back to front no more than ½" (1.3 cm) from where the yarn last came out. Insert the needle from front to back at the point where the first stitch began, then bring the needle back through to the front, the same distance along the edge as before.

2 Work in backstitch from right to left along the whole seam, making sure that you stay close to the edge and go through both pieces of fabric. Secure the end with a couple of overlapping stitches.

Woven seam

Place the pieces to be joined side by side on a flat surface, with wrong sides facing up and edges together. Thread a large blunt-ended sewing needle with yarn. Starting at the bottom and working from right to left, place the needle under the loop of the first stitch on both pieces and draw the yarn through. Move up one stitch and repeat this process going from left to right. Continue to zigzag loosely from edge to edge. Pull the yarn tight every inch (2.5 cm) or so, allowing the edges to join together. A woven seam gives a flatter finish than a backstitch seam and works better when sewing together baby garments and fine work.

Single crochet seam

Place the pieces to be joined right sides together. Using a crochet hook and working from right to left, work a row of single crochet stitches through both layers (see page 21).

Slip stitch seam

Joining pieces by slip stitching them together with a crochet hook makes a firm seam with an attractive ridge on the right side. Place the pieces wrong sides together and work a row of slip stitch through both layers (see page 21).

Edge finishes

Edge finishes can be worked directly into the crochet fabric. Single crochet edging is used mainly for finishing necklines and borders on garments and it can be worked in a contrasting color of yarn. Crab stitch edging is more hard-wearing due to the small knots of yarn made along the row. It can be worked directly into the edge of a piece of crochet fabric, as shown, or several rows of single crochet can be worked first to act as a foundation. Picot edgings offer a more decorative finish.

Single crochet edging

Single crochet is a useful and flexible edge finish. Working from right to left, make a row of ordinary single crochet stitches (see page 21) into the edge of the crochet fabric, spacing the stitches evenly along the edge.

Crab stitch edging

Also known as reverse single crochet, this stitch makes a strong, fairly rigid edging with an attractive texture. Unlike most other crochet techniques, this stitch is worked from left to right along the row

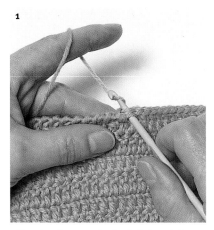

1 Keeping the yarn to the left, insert the hook from front to back into the next stitch and wrap the yarn over the hook.

2 Draw the loop through the stitch from back to front so that there are now two loops on the hook. Finish by wrapping the yarn over the hook again, then draw the yarn through both loops to complete the stitch.

Picot edging

This stitch makes a delicate edge with tiny protruding loops of yarn. Work a foundation row of single crochet and then turn the work.

1 Work three chain stitches, then work a slip stitch into the third chain from the hook. This makes one picot.

2 Skip the next stitch, then work a slip stitch into the following stitch. Repeat from the beginning of step 1 and continue doing so all along the edge.

Pompons

Pompons are very easy to make using a pompon maker or circles of cardboard. If you are using cardboard, cut out two circles about 1" (2.5 cm) larger than the pompon you want to make. Cut out a central 1" (2.5 cm) hole.

1 Thread a large blunt-ended needle with as many ends of yarn as it will take; the yarn ends should be about 3' (1 m) long.

2 Hold the two disks of the pompon maker together (or the two circles of cardboard) and thread the needle through the center, around the outside, and back through the center from the front, holding the tail end of yarn in place with your thumb if need be. Continue to do this until the central hole is full.

Pompons are the perfect finishing touch for this scarf (pages 98–9), or you could add them to other projects if you wish.

3 Push the blade of a sharp pair of scissors between the 2 disks and cut around the pompon.

4 Tie a piece of yarn around the center of the pompon as tightly as possible. Remove the disks and trim the pompon to form a neat ball.

Cords

Crochet cords make attractive straps for purses, ties to secure a neckline or other crochet pieces, or several lengths can be sewn onto a plain piece of crochet to decorate it with shapes such as spirals, stripes, or swirls.

Single slip stitch cord

Work a foundation chain to the required length. Insert the hook into the second chain from the hook and work a row of slip stitches (see page 21) along one side of the chain.

Double slip stitch cord

Work a foundation chain to the required length. Insert the hook into the second chain from the hook and work a row of slip stitches along each side of the chain, adding an extra chain stitch at the end of the first side as a turning chain.

Single crochet cord

1 Work a foundation chain to the required length. Insert the hook into the second chain from the hook and work a row of single crochet stitches (see page 21) along one side of the chain.

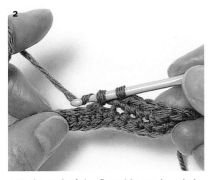

2 At the end of the first side, work a chain stitch as a turning chain, then work along the second side of the chain in single crochet as before.

BELOW LEFT: SINGLE SLIP STITCH CORD
MIDDLE: DOUBLE SLIP STITCH CORD
RIGHT: SINGLE CROCHET CORD

Buttons

Finishing touches such as buttons are very important to the look of your finished accessories. If you cannot find anything suitable, try crocheting a ball button using a complementary yarn to the main project. Refer to page 30 if you need an explanation of the abbreviations used here.

1 Work a ball button over a bead or a small ball of batting. Using a smaller hook than suggested for the yarn you are using, ch 2, then work 4 sc into the first ch. Without joining or turning the work, work 2 sc into each stitch made on the previous round. For every following increase round, work *1 sc into first st, 2 sc into next stitch; repeat from * until the piece covers one half of the bead or ball of batting.

2 Slip the bead or ball into the crochet cover. Start decreasing by working *1 sc into next st, then sc 2 sts together; repeat from * until the bead or ball of batting is completely covered.

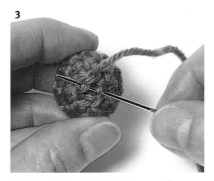

3 Break off the yarn, leaving an end about 12" (30 cm) long. Thread the yarn into a large blunt-ended needle and work a few stitches to secure. Do not cut the yarn; instead use it to attach the button to the garment.

Several projects use crocheted cords, including this fun and quirky scarf made up of bobbles on a string (pages 94–5).

quick-and-easy
bags & purses

WHAT COULD BE MORE REWARDING THAN CREATING THESE FANTASTIC BAGS

AND PURSES. EACH PROJECT CAN EASILY BE CREATED IN AN EVENING OR

TWO, AND THEY ARE IDEAL FOR PRACTICING NEW TECHNIQUES. FOR EXAMPLE,

LEARN HOW TO FELT WITH THE SLASH-HANDLED BAG, PRACTICE YOUR STITCH

TECHNIQUES WITH THE BIG SHOPPING BAG AND ACID-BRIGHT ZIGZAG BAG, OR

MAKE THE BULB BAG AND EVENING PURSES TO HONE YOUR SHAPING SKILLS.

Project 1: Slash-handled bag

This up-to-the-minute bag is practical but fashionable, with its bright stripe formation and textured felted fabric. The bag is worked in stripes of six colors, but you could easily use just one color or limit yourself to a palette of two or three colors. Alternatively, you could use a different color for each stripe, which is a great way to use up scraps of yarn. Just make sure that the yarns you use are all the same weight and that the fibers will felt— that is, not cotton, superwash wool, or synthetic yarns.

TIP: MAKE IT BIGGER

The size of the bag can easily be altered by reducing or increasing the number of stitches and rows.

PANELS (MAKE 2)

Foundation chain: Using a size F (4 mm) hook and yarn A, ch 50.

Row 1 (RS): Ch 1, 1 sc into 2nd ch from hook, 1 sc into every ch to end.

Rows 2–4: Repeat row 1.

Rows 1–4 form a single stripe.

Rows 5–8: Change to yarn B and repeat rows 1–4.

Rows 9–24: Repeat rows 1–4 using each of the remaining yarns in turn.

Rows 25–48: Repeat rows 1–24, using the same sequence of six yarns.

Rows 49–56: Repeat rows 1–4 using yarn A, then using yarn B.

To work the handle, change to yarn C.

Row 57: Ch 1, 14 sc, ch 22, skip next 22 sc, 14 sc.

Row 58–60: Repeat row 1 using yarn C.

Rows 61–68: Repeat rows 1–4 using yarn D, then using yarn E.

FINISHING

Weave in any loose ends. With right sides together, backstitch the panels around the sides and base, making sure that the stripes align. Felt the bag.

before you start

MATERIALS

DK-weight yarn (100% pure new wool; approx. 124 yds/113 m per 2 oz/50 g ball) in 6 colors:

A Orange x 1 ball
B Turquoise x 1 ball
C Red x 1 ball
D Pink x 1 ball
E Lime x 1 ball
F Ecru x 1 ball

HOOK SIZE

F (4 mm)

GAUGE

17 sts x 20 rows = 4" (10 cm) in single crochet before felting

FINISHED SIZE

11" (29 cm) wide x 14" (35 cm) long before felting
10" (25 cm) wide x 12½" (32 cm) long after felting

KEY TECHNIQUES

- Foundation chains, pages 19–20
- Single crochet, page 21
- Joining a new color, page 24
- Seams, pages 33–4
- Felting, page 41

ABBREVIATIONS

ch—chain
RS—right side
sc—single crochet
st(s)—stitch(es)

The six stripes of different colors mean this bag will go with lots of outfits, while the felting process makes the fabric strong and sturdy.

New skills/felting

This is a process of shrinking a woolen fabric by washing it in soapy water to bind the fibers together to create a more solid and fluffy fabric. It can be done by hand but is easier in a washing machine. Felting is very much a case of trial and error, because each washing machine varies. Always experiment with a crocheted swatch before placing the finished item into the machine.

1 Gently brush the fabric with a spiky piece of Velcro to fluff up the surface. Loosening the fibers in this way will help them to bind together.

2 Place the finished item in a washing machine with a hard-wearing fabric such as an old pair of jeans or a denim jacket (if using a dark color yarn) or a few old tennis balls. Add a small amount of your usual washing detergent and wash on your machine's hottest cycle. The felting may require more than one cycle to reach the desired stage.

3 When the cycle is complete, ease the damp item into the required shape by patting, pulling, and smoothing as necessary. Allow to air dry.

Project 2: Acid-bright zigzag bag

Bright and funky colors accentuate the jazzy zigzag pattern of the front panel of this bag to produce a textural mix of solid blocks and extending rays. The back panel is very easy to work, featuring large blocks of just two colors.

FRONT PANEL

Foundation chain: Using a size G (4.5 mm) hook and yarn A, ch 36.

Row 1 (RS): Ch 1, 1 sc into 2nd ch from hook, 1 sc into every ch to end.

Row 2: Ch 1, 1 sc into every sc to end.

Rows 3–6: Repeat row 2.

Change to yarn B.

Row 7: Ch 1, *1 sc into next st, 1 sc into next st 2 rows down fabric, 1 sc into next st 3 rows down fabric, 1 sc into next st 4 rows down fabric, 1 sc into next st 5 rows down fabric, 1 sc into next st 6 rows down fabric, repeat from * to end.

Rows 8–12: Repeat row 2.

Change to yarn C.

Row 13: Ch 1, *1 sc into next st 6 rows down fabric, 1 sc into next st 5 rows down fabric, 1 sc into next st 4 rows down fabric, 1 sc into next st 3 rows down fabric, 1 sc into next st 2 rows down fabric, 1 sc into next st, repeat from * to end.

Rows 14–18: Repeat row 2.

Change to yarn D.

Rows 19–24: Repeat rows 7–12.

Change to yarn E.

Rows 25–30: Repeat rows 13–18.

Rows 31–42: Repeat rows 1–12.

SHAPING THE OPENING

Change to yarn C.

Row 43: Repeat row 7.

Row 44: Ch 1, 1 sc into every sc to end.

Row 45: Ch 1, dec 1, 1 sc into every sc to last 2 sts, dec 1 (34 sts).

Row 46: Repeat row 44.

Row 47: Repeat row 45 (32 sts).

Row 48: Repeat row 44.

Change to yarn D.

Row 49: Ch 1, 1 sc into next st 4 rows down fabric, 1 sc into next st 3 rows down fabric, 1 sc into next st 2 rows down fabric, 1 sc into next st, *1 sc into next st 6 rows down fabric, 1 sc into next st 5 rows down fabric, 1 sc into next st 4 rows down fabric, 1 sc into next st 3 rows down fabric, 1 sc into next st 2 rows down fabric, 1 sc into next st, repeat from * to end, finishing with 1 sc 3 rows down fabric.

Rows 50–54: Repeat rows 44–48 (28 sts).

Change to yarn E.

Row 55: Ch 1, 1 sc into next st 4 rows down fabric, 1 sc into next st 5 rows down fabric, 1 sc into next st 6 rows down fabric, *1 sc into next st, 1 sc into next st 2 rows down fabric, 1 sc into next st 3 rows down fabric, 1 sc into next st 4 rows down fabric, 1 sc into next st 5 rows down fabric, 1 sc into next st 6 rows down fabric, repeat from * to end, finishing with 1 sc 2 rows down fabric.

Rows 56–60: Repeat rows 44–48 (24 sts).

before you start

MATERIALS

DK-weight yarn (100% cotton; approx. 93 yds/85 m per 2 oz/50 g ball) in 5 colors:

A Purple x 2 balls

B Turquoise x 1 ball

C Pink x 1 ball

D Yellow x 1 ball

E Orange x 1 ball

Two bamboo handles, approx. 6" (15 cm) wide at base

HOOK SIZE

G (4.5 mm)

GAUGE

13 sts x 24 rows = 4" (10 cm) in zigzag pattern

14 sts x 17 rows = 4" (10 cm) in single crochet

FINISHED SIZE

10" (25 cm) high x 9½" (24 cm) wide

KEY TECHNIQUES

• Foundation chains, pages 19–20

• Single crochet, page 21

• Shaping techniques, pages 26–7

• Seams, pages 33–4

ABBREVIATIONS

ch—chain

dec 1—decrease 1 stitch as follows: place hook into first sc, yo and pull through, place hook into next sc, yo and pull through (3 loops on hook), yo and pull through all 3 loops on hook

RS—right side

sc—single crochet

st(s)—stitch(es)

yo—yarn over

project 2: acid-bright zigzag bag

Change to yarn A.

Row 61: Ch 1, *1 sc into next st 6 rows down fabric, 1 sc into next st 5 rows down fabric, 1 sc into next st 4 rows down fabric, 1 sc into next st 3 rows down fabric, 1 sc into next st 2 rows down fabric, 1 sc into next st, repeat from * to end.

Row 62: Ch 1, 1 sc into every sc to end.

Rows 63–68: Repeat row 62.

Fasten off.

BACK PANEL

Foundation chain: Using a size G (4.5 mm) hook and yarn A, ch 36.

Row 1 (RS): Ch 1, 1 sc into 2nd ch from hook, 1 sc into every ch to end.

Row 2: Ch 1, 1 sc into every sc to end.

Rows 3–6: Repeat row 2.

Change to yarn B.

Row 7–32: Repeat row 2.

Change to yarn A.

SHAPING THE OPENING

Row 33: Ch 1, 1 sc into every sc to end.

Row 34: Ch 1, dec 1, 1 sc into every sc to last 2 sts, dec 1 (34 sts).

Rows 35–44: Repeat rows 33–34 (24 sts).

Row 45: Ch 1, 1 sc into every sc to end.

Rows 46–51: Repeat row 45.

Fasten off yarn.

FINISHING

Weave in any loose ends, then block and press the panels to the correct size. With right sides together, backstitch the panels around the sides and base. Attach a handle to each panel by looping the top edge of the fabric around the handle, from outside to inside. Sew the edge of the fabric to the inside of the panel.

If acid-bright colors are not to your taste, this bag would look just as good in natural or more muted shades.

TIP: ZIGZAG STITCH

The zigzag stitch (first used in row 7 of the front panel) is very easy to work, but it is important that you do not pull the yarn too tightly or it will not lie correctly.

Project 3: Bulb bag

This cute little ball-shaped bag is the perfect size for carrying a change purse, keys, and other small essentials. The round shape is created in four separate pieces that are then sewn together. The bag is worked in strong cotton yarn in a single crochet stitch to give a dense and sturdy fabric, helping to keep its shape, while the zipper opening allows easy access.

before you start

MATERIALS

DK-weight yarn (100% cotton; approx. 93 yds/85 m per 2 oz/50 g ball) x 2 balls (purple)
6" (15 cm) closed-end zipper
⅞" (22 cm) diameter shell button

HOOK SIZE

F (4 mm)

GAUGE

15 sts x 20 rows = 4" (10 cm) in single crochet

FINISHED SIZE

7" (18 cm) diameter

KEY TECHNIQUES

- Foundation chains, pages 19–20
- Single crochet, page 21
- Shaping techniques, pages 26–7
- Seams, pages 33–4
- Inserting a zipper, page 45

ABBREVIATIONS

ch—chain

dec 1—decrease 1 stitch as follows: place hook into first sc, yo and pull through, place hook into next sc, yo and pull through (3 loops on hook), yo and pull through all 3 loops on hook

inc 1—increase 1 stitch as follows: 2 sc into next sc

RS—right side

sc—single crochet

st(s)—stitch(es)

yo—yarn over

PANELS (MAKE 4)

Foundation chain: Using a size F (4 mm) hook, ch 3.

Row 1 (RS): Ch 1, 1 sc into every ch to end.

Row 2: Ch 1, inc 1, 1 sc, inc 1 (5 sts).

Row 3: Ch 1, inc 1, 3 sc, inc 1 (7 sts).

Row 4: Ch 1, inc 1, 5 sc, inc 1 (9 sts).

Row 5: Ch 1, inc 1, 7 sc, inc 1 (11 sts).

Row 6: Ch 1, inc 1, 9 sc, inc 1 (13 sts).

Row 7: Ch 1, inc 1, 11 sc, inc 1 (15 sts).

Rows 8–18: Ch 1, 1 sc into every sc to end.

Row 19: Ch 1, dec 1, 11 sc, dec 1 (13 sts).

Row 20: Ch 1, dec 1, 9 sc, dec 1 (11 sts).

Row 21: Ch 1, dec 1, 7 sc, dec 1 (9 sts).

Row 22: Ch 1, dec 1, 5 sc, dec 1 (7 sts).

Row 23: Ch 1, dec 1, 3 sc, dec 1 (5 sts).

Row 24: Ch 1, dec 1, 1 sc, dec 1 (3 sts).

Fasten off yarn.

SEWING UP

With right sides together, backstitch the side seams of the panels, but leave one side open for the zipper. Sew the zipper in place, then sew the openings at the top and bottom of the bag closed.

WRIST STRAP

Foundation chain: Using a size F (4 mm) hook, ch 7.

Row 1 (RS): Ch 1, 1 sc into every ch to end.

Row 2: Ch 1, 1 sc into every sc to end.

Repeat row 2 until the handle measures approx. 8½" (21 cm) long.

Make a buttonhole as follows:

Next 3 rows: Ch 1, 3 sc, turn.

Break off yarn and rejoin at 5th sc of main strap and repeat previous 3 rows.

Next row: Ch 1, 1 sc into every st to end.

Repeat last row once more.

Fasten off yarn.

FINISHING

Weave in any loose ends. Sew a button on the opposite end of the wrist strap from the buttonhole. Sew the strap to the bag on the opposite seam from the zipper, approximately 8 rows in from the button end of the strap.

If you prefer, you could lengthen the wrist strap so that the bag can be worn across the shoulders instead.

New skills/inserting a zipper

Inserting a zipper can seem like a tricky process, but if you take your time and try not to stretch the fabric, it is actually easy to do.

1 Pin the zipper into position, then baste in place using a sewing needle and thread.

2 Backstitch the zipper into place, using the crocheted stitches as a guideline to keep the backstitches straight. Use a matching color sewing thread, or, depending on the yarn you are using, you may be able to split it into strands that you can use for sewing.

Project 4: Big shopping bag

Fed up with having to carry lots of bags around with you, juggling things from hand to hand? Well, this is the bag for you. It is big enough to carry everything you really need and much more besides. The main body of the bag is made from two rectangular panels, with the handles worked separately and then stitched into position.

PANELS (MAKE 2)

Foundation chain: Using a size N (9 mm) hook and yarn A, ch 26.

Row 1 (RS): Ch 1, 1 sc into 2nd ch from hook, 1 sc into every ch to end.

Row 2: Ch 1, 1 sc into 2nd sc from hook, 1 sc into back loop of every sc to end.

Row 3: Ch 1, 1 sc into 2nd sc from hook, 1 sc into front loop of every sc to end.

Rows 2–3 form the fabric pattern. Repeat another 23 times or until the required length is achieved.

Fasten off yarn.

SEWING UP

Turn the panels sidewise so that the rows of single crochet run vertically. With right sides together, backstitch the panels around the sides and base.

CONTRAST BORDER

Foundation round: Using a size P (10 mm) hook and yarn B, and with RS facing,

46 sc around the top opening of the bag, then sl st into first sc.

Round 1: Ch 1, 1 sc into 2nd st from hook, 1 sc into every sc to end, sl st into ch 1 at beginning of row.

Rounds 2–4: Repeat round 1 three times. Fasten off yarn.

HANDLES (MAKE 2)

Foundation chain: Using a size P (10 mm) hook and yarn B, ch 5.

Row 1 (RS): Ch 1, 1 sc into 2nd ch from hook, 1 sc into every ch to end.

Row 2: Ch 1, 1 sc into 2nd sc from hook, 1 sc into every sc to end.

Repeat row 2 another 28 times or until the required length is achieved.

FINISHING

Weave in any loose ends. Pin the handles to the outside of the bag, so that the ends of the handles extend across the contrast border as far as the main panels, and then backstitch into place.

before you start

MATERIALS

A Super bulky-weight yarn (100% merino wool; approx. 87 yds/80 m per 4 oz/100 g ball) x 2 balls (purple)

B Extra super bulky-weight yarn (100% merino wool; approx. 33 yds/30 m per 4 oz/100 g ball) x 2 balls (pink)

HOOK SIZE

N (9 mm), P (10 mm)

GAUGE

10 sts x 9 rows = 4" (10 cm) in panel pattern

FINISHED SIZE

12" (30 cm) wide x 13" (33 cm) long excluding handles

KEY TECHNIQUES

• Foundation chains, pages 19–20
• Single crochet, page 21
• Seams, pages 33–4

ABBREVIATIONS

ch—chain
RS—right side
sc—single crochet
sl st—slip stitch
st(s)—stitch(es)

This simple design is enhanced by the use of bulky yarns to make a prominent feature of the stitch pattern. This is accentuated by joining the pieces so that the stitch patterns run at different angles.

Project 5: Evening purses

This stylish duo of neck and shoulder purses made from sparkly metallic yarn are ideal for the evening wear, but you could make them using cotton yarn for daytime use if you prefer.

NECK PURSE

Foundation chain: Using a size E (3.5 mm) hook and yarn A doubled, ch 20.

Row 1 (RS): Ch 1, 1 sc into 2nd ch from hook, 1 sc into every ch to end.

Row 2: Ch 1, 1 sc into every sc to end.

Repeat row 2 until work measures 8" (20 cm), ending with a WS row.

FLAP

Next row (RS): Ch 1, skip first sc to decrease 1 stitch, 1 sc into every sc to end (19 sc).

Repeat this row until 2 sts remain.

Fasten off yarn, leaving a long end to make a button loop.

before you start

MATERIALS
Light-weight yarn (80% viscose, 20% polyester; approx. 104 yds/95 m per 1 oz/25 g ball) in 2 colors:
A Gray x 2 balls (neck purse)
B Blue x 4 balls (shoulder purse)
Yarns are used doubled throughout
1 decorative button per purse

HOOK SIZE
C (3 mm), E (3.5 mm)

GAUGE
22 sts x 24 rows = 4" (10 cm) in single crochet using a size C (3 mm) hook and yarn doubled
20 sts x 15 rows = 4" (10 cm) in half double crochet using a size E (3.5 mm) hook and yarn doubled

FINISHED SIZE
Neck purse: 4" (10 cm) square
Shoulder purse: 6" (15 cm) wide x 7½" (19 cm) long

KEY TECHNIQUES
• Foundation chains, pages 19–20
• Single crochet, page 21
• Half double crochet, page 23
• Seams, pages 33–4

ABBREVIATIONS
ch—chain
hdc—half double crochet
RS—right side
sc—single crochet
sl st—slip stitch
st(s)—stitch(es)
WS—wrong side

These little purses are just big enough to hold your essentials for a night out, and in sparkly yarn they add the finishing touch to a glamorous outfit.

CORD

Foundation chain: Using a size E (3.5 mm) hook and yarn A doubled, make a foundation chain about 2" (5 cm) longer than required. Change to a size C (3 mm) hook and work a row of sl st along one side of the chain. Fasten off yarn.

SHOULDER PURSE

Foundation chain: Using a size E (3.5 mm) hook and yarn B doubled, ch 29.
Row 1 (RS): Ch 2, 1 hdc into 3rd ch from hook, 1 hdc into every ch to end.
Row 2: Ch 2, 1 hdc into every st to end, 1 hdc into 2nd ch of ch 2.
Repeat row 2 until work measures 15" (38 cm), ending with a WS row.

FLAP

Next row (RS): Ch 2, 1 hdc into first 2 hdc, skip 1 st, 1 hdc into every st to last 3 sts, skip 1 st, 1 hdc into next st, 1 hdc into 2nd ch of ch 2.
Repeat this row until 4 sts remain.
Next row: Ch 1, 1 sc into every st to end. Fasten off yarn, leaving a long end to make a button loop.

CORD

Make a cord using yarn B in the same way as for the neck purse, but work the row of sl st along both sides of the chain instead of just one side. Fasten off yarn.

FINISHING

Weave in any loose ends. For both purses, fold the main body of the purse right sides together and backstitch the side seams. Use the yarn end at the point of the flap to crochet a chain long enough to form a button loop. Join the end of the chain to the point of the flap with a slip stitch. Fold over the flap and sew a button onto the purse to correspond with the loop. Sew the cord to the side seams of the purse so that the ends of the cord extend 2" (5 cm) inside the purse.

quick-and-easy throws & pillows

CROCHET FABRICS MAKE WONDERFUL SOFT FURNISHINGS FOR THE HOME. THE

RUFFLE THROW BRINGS THE TRADITIONAL CANDLEWICK BEDSPREAD INTO THE

21ST CENTURY, AND THE IDEA HAS BEEN ADAPTED TO MAKE A RUFFLE PILLOW.

THE SOFTLY TEXTURED THROW AND PILLOW FRAMED BY LUXURIOUS TASSEL

FRINGING WILL MAKE ANY HOME FEEL WARM AND WELCOMING. YOU CAN ALSO

HAVE LOTS OF FUN WITH COLOR BY MAKING THE FUNKY FLOOR PILLOW.

Project 6: Softly textured throw

A modern classic, this simple throw is worked in the easiest of stitches and bordered with complementary colored tassels made from thick merino wool. The main panel of the throw is crocheted in a soft and light lambswool and mohair blend yarn in a neutral shade, making it both versatile and practical.

PANEL

Foundation chain: Using a size J (6 mm) hook and yarn A, ch 132.

Row 1 (RS): Ch 3, 1 dc into 4th ch from hook, 1 dc into every ch to end.

Row 2: Ch 3, 1 dc into every dc to end. Row 2 forms the pattern. Repeat this row 107 times or until the required length is achieved.

FINISHING

Weave in any loose ends, then block and press to the correct size. Cut 10" (25 cm) lengths of yarn B and add the tassel fringe, starting between the first and second stitches at one corner and then working all the way around the throw.

New skills/tassel fringe

A tassel fringe is a great way to add an interesting but simple edge to a crocheted project. A complementary yarn or color can be used to enhance the fringe as a design feature.

1 Cut pieces of yarn to the required length. Placing the hook through the fabric in the required place, fold a length of yarn in half, and place it around the hook. For bulkier tassels, use several lengths per tassel.

2 Pull the loop of yarn through toward yourself.

3 Insert the ends of the tassel through the loop and pull tight. Continue adding tassels evenly around the edge.

before you start

MATERIALS

A Aran-weight yarn (70% lambswool, 26% kid mohair, 4% nylon; approx. 153 yds/140 m per 2 oz/50 g ball) x 12 balls (beige)

B Extra super bulky-weight yarn (100% merino wool; approx. 33 yds/30 m per 4 oz/100 g ball) x 3 balls (cream)

HOOK SIZE

J (6 mm)

GAUGE

11 sts x 7 rows = 4" (10 cm) in double crochet

FINISHED SIZE

48 x 60" (123 x 154 cm) excluding tassels

KEY TECHNIQUES

• Foundation chains, pages 19–20
• Double crochet, pages 22–3
• Tassel fringe, page 52

ABBREVIATIONS

ch—chain
dc—double crochet
RS—right side
st(s)—stitch(es)

This delightfully soft lambswool, mohair, and merino wool throw is perfect for keeping you warm, and its neutral colors will complement any home decor scheme.

Project 7: Softly textured pillow

This soft and cuddly pillow is crocheted in a lambswool and kid mohair blend yarn, with thick merino wool tassels. The pillow is worked throughout in a basic double crochet stitch, and the lightly brushed tassels and delicate shell buttons add the perfect finishing touches.

BACK PANEL

Foundation chain: Using a size J (6 mm) hook and yarn A, ch 50.
Row 1 (RS): Ch 3, 1 dc into 4th ch from hook, 1 dc into every ch to end.
Row 2: Ch 3, 1 dc into every dc to end. Repeat row 2 another 22 times. Fasten off yarn.

FRONT PANEL

Rejoin yarn A at the foundation chain of the back panel.
Row 1 (RS): Ch 3, 1 dc into every dc to end. Work to match the back panel, then add an extra 8 rows for the flap. Fasten off the yarn.

FINISHING

Weave in any loose ends, then block and press to the correct size. Fold the panels wrong sides together at the foundation chain, so that the front panel flap overlaps the back panel. Using a size J (6 mm) hook and yarn A, join the side seams with single crochet. Cut 12" (30 cm) lengths of yarn B and add the tassel fringe, starting at a corner of one of the side seams. Make sure the tassels are positioned around the fold of the flap, not on the edge of the flap. Lightly brush the tassels to make them more fluffy. Sew five buttons evenly spaced across the back panel about 1–2" (2.5–5 cm) below the edge of the flap. Make button loops to match the button positions by working a chain from the edge of the flap and joining the other end of the chain to the flap with a slip stitch to form a loop. Insert a pillow form and fasten the button loops.

before you start

MATERIALS

A Aran-weight yarn (70% lambswool, 26% kid mohair, 4% nylon; approx. 153 yds/140 m per 2 oz/50 g ball) x 4 balls (brown)
B Extra super bulky-weight yarn (100% merino wool; approx. 33 yds/30 m per 4 oz/100 g ball) x 2 balls (multi-beige)
5 large shell buttons
16" (40 cm) square pillow form

HOOK SIZE

J (6 mm)

GAUGE

12 repeats x 6 rows = 4" (10 cm) in double crochet using yarn A

FINISHED SIZE

16" (40 cm) square

KEY TECHNIQUES

• Foundation chains, pages 19–20
• Double crochet, pages 22–3
• Seams, pages 33–4
• Tassel fringe, page 52

ABBREVIATIONS

ch—chain
dc—double crochet
RS—right side
st(s)—stitch(es)

The multicolored yarn used for the tassels increases the soft textural appeal of this pillow. The plain panels are the perfect foil for the tassels and decorative shell buttons.

Project 8: Ruffle throw

This throw is a modern interpretation of a traditional candlewick bedspread, using a wonderfully light and soft lambswool and kid mohair blend yarn. The throw is worked as three separate panels so that it is easier to handle, then the textured ruffles are worked onto the fabric in evenly spaced rows.

PANELS (MAKE 3)

Foundation chain: Using a size J (6 mm) hook, ch 50.

Row 1 (RS): Ch 3, 1 dc into 4th ch from hook, *ch 1, skip 1 ch, 1 dc, repeat from * to end.

Row 2: Ch 2, 1 dc into first ch space, *ch 1, 1 dc into next ch space, repeat from * to end.

Repeat row 2 another 64 times or until the required length is achieved.

Fasten off yarn.

RUFFLES

Join the three panels together using a woven seam. Using a size J (6 mm) hook and with right side facing, join the yarn at one of the lower corners of the throw with a slip stitch. Work a single row of ruffles vertically up the throw. Continue adding rows of ruffles, each row 5 spaces apart, until you have worked 16 rows of ruffles in total. Fasten off the yarn.

FINISHING

Weave in any loose ends, then block and press to the correct size.

before you start

MATERIALS

Aran-weight yarn (70% lambswool, 26% kid mohair, 4% nylon; approx. 153 yds/140 m per 2 oz/50 g ball) x 12 balls (cream)

HOOK SIZE

J (6 mm)

GAUGE

7 rows x 7 (1 dc, ch 1) pattern repeats = 4" (10 cm), but an accurate gauge is not important

FINISHED SIZE

47" (120 cm) square

KEY TECHNIQUES

- Foundation chains, pages 19–20
- Double crochet, pages 22–3
- Seams, pages 33–4
- Single-row ruffles, page 58

ABBREVIATIONS

ch—chain
dc—double crochet
RS—right side
sl st—slip stitch
st(s)—stitch(es)

Multipurpose accessories are always a great bonus. Use this throw as a soft furnishing in your home or wear it as a shawl in chilly weather—it will look great either way.

The stitch used to make the panels of the throw leaves part of the loop unworked; this can be used to work a ruffle.

1 To work the first row of ruffles, join the yarn as instructed in the main pattern. Ch 6, sl st into first ch space along edge of fabric.

2 *Ch 6, sl st into top of dc, ch 6, sl st into first ch space, repeat from * to end.

3 To work additional rows of ruffles, join the yarn as instructed in the main pattern. **Ch 6, sl st around stem of next dc in row above, ch 6, sl st around same dc, repeat from ** until you reach the top edge of the throw. Fasten off yarn.

Project 9: Ruffle pillow

This pillow is delightfully tactile. The front and back panels of the pillow are worked separately, and then blocks of ruffles are crocheted onto the front panel using a simple chain stitch to create highly textured stripes.

before you start

MATERIALS

Aran-weight yarn (70% lambswool, 26% kid mohair, 4% nylon; approx. 153 yds/140 m per 2 oz/50 g ball) x 5 balls (blue)
4 large shell buttons
12" (30 cm) square pillow form

HOOK SIZE

J (6 mm)

GAUGE

19 sts x 10 rows = 4" (10 cm) in half double crochet

FINISHED SIZE

12" (30 cm) square

KEY TECHNIQUES

• Foundation chains, pages 19–20
• Single crochet, page 21
• Half double crochet, page 23
• Seams, pages 33–4
• Blocks of ruffles, page 60

ABBREVIATIONS

ch—chain
hdc—half double crochet
RS—right side
sc—single crochet
st(s)—stitch(es)

BACK PANEL

Foundation chain: Using a size J (6 mm) hook, ch 40.
Row 1 (RS): Ch 2, 1 hdc into 3rd ch from hook, 1 hdc into every ch to end.
Row 2: Ch 2, 1 hdc into every hdc to end.
Rows 3–36: Repeat row 2 another 34 times.

FRONT PANEL

Foundation chain: Using a size J (6 mm) hook, ch 50.
Row 1: Ch 2, 1 hdc into 3rd ch from hook, 1 hdc into every ch to end.
Row 2 (RS): Ch 2, *1 hdc into back loop of every hdc to end.
Row 3: Ch 2, *1 hdc into front loop of every hdc to end.
Rows 2–3 form the pattern.
Rows 4–49: Repeat rows 2–3 another 23 times.

RUFFLES

Using a size J (6 mm) hook and with the right side of the front panel facing, join the yarn at the bottom right corner by placing the hook under the front loop of the first stitch. Work rows of ruffles vertically up the panel in blocks of four. Space the blocks of ruffles at three-row intervals until you have worked four blocks of ruffles in total. Fasten off the yarn.

FINISHING

Weave in any loose ends, then block and press to the correct size. Place the two panels right sides together with the ruffles positioned vertically; about 4" (10 cm) of the front panel should extend beyond the back panel to be used for the pillow flap. Backstitch the pieces together. Turn right side out and sew four buttons evenly spaced across the back panel about 1–2" (2.5–5 cm) below the edge of the flap. Insert a pillow form and use the last ruffle of each block as a fastening loop for the buttons.

New skills/blocks of ruffles

The stitch used to make the front panel leaves part of the loop unworked; this can be used to work a ruffle. The ruffles are worked in blocks of four.

1 To work the first block of ruffles, join the yarn as instructed in the main pattern. *Ch 6, 1 sc under next front loop, repeat from * to end. Fasten off yarn.

2 Move along one row and rejoin the yarn. *Ch 6, 1 sc under next back loop, repeat from * to end. Fasten off yarn.

3 Moving along one row at a time, repeat steps 1–2 to complete the first block of ruffles. Continue working blocks of ruffles in this way, spacing them as instructed in the main pattern (in this pillow, three rows apart).

The beauty of crocheted fabrics often lies in their textural appeal. This pillow combines a fluffy mohair and lambswool yarn with thick ruffles to wonderful effect.

Project 10: Funky floor pillow

This colorful pillow is big, bouncy, and fabulously funky. Kids and adults alike will enjoy using it during all those times when you feel like stretching out on the floor watching TV or lounging around chatting to friends. It is extremely easy to make, and because the front is worked as a series of smaller panels, it is also a great piece of portable crochet.

before you start

MATERIALS

Bulky-weight yarn (42% merino wool, 30% acrylic, 28% superfine alpaca; 109 yds/100 m per 4 oz/100 g ball) in 7 colors:

A Beige marl x 1 ball
B Orange marl x 1 ball
C Blue/green marl x 1 ball
D Purple marl x 1 ball
E Dark blue marl x 1 ball
F Red marl x 1 ball
G Black/gray marl x 4 balls
28" (72 cm) square pillow form

HOOK SIZE

L (8 mm)

GAUGE

8 sts x 6 rows = 4" (10 cm) in double crochet

FINISHED SIZE

28" (72 cm) square

KEY TECHNIQUES

• Foundation chains, pages 19–20
• Double crochet, pages 22–3
• Seams, pages 33–4

ABBREVIATIONS

ch—chain
dc—double crochet
RS—right side
st(s)—stitch(es)

FIRST FRONT PANEL

Foundation chain: Using a size L (8 mm) hook and yarn A, ch 28.
Row 1 (RS): Ch 3, 1 dc into 4th ch from hook, 1 dc into every ch to end.
Row 2: Ch 3, 1 dc into every dc to end.
Rows 3–5: Repeat row 2.
Change to yarn B.
Rows 6–10: Repeat row 2.
Change to yarn C.
Rows 11–15: Repeat row 2.
Change to yarn D.
Rows 16–20: Repeat row 2.
Fasten off yarn.

SECOND FRONT PANEL

Work as for the first front panel in the following stripe sequence.
Rows 1–5: Yarn C.
Rows 6–10: Yarn B.
Rows 11–15: Yarn E.
Rows 16–20: Yarn F.

THIRD FRONT PANEL

Work as for the first front panel in the following stripe sequence.
Rows 1–5: Yarn D.
Rows 6–10: Yarn B.
Rows 11–15: Yarn A.
Rows 16–20: Yarn E.

FOURTH FRONT PANEL

Work as for the first front panel in the following stripe sequence.
Rows 1–5: Yarn A.
Rows 6–10: Yarn C.
Rows 11–15: Yarn D.
Rows 16–20: Yarn G.

BACK PANEL

Foundation chain: Using a size L (8 mm) hook and yarn G, ch 56.
Row 1 (RS): Ch 3, 1 dc into 4th ch from hook, 1 dc into every ch to end.
Row 2: Ch 3, 1 dc into every dc to end.
Rows 3–40: Repeat row 2 another 38 times.
Fasten off yarn.

FINISHING

Weave in any loose ends, then block and press the pieces. Place the outer edge of first front panel wrong sides together with fastening off edge of second front panel so that the stripes are running horizontal against vertical. Using a size L (8 mm) hook and yarn G, join the panels using single crochet. Repeat to join all the front panels together, rotating the stripes as shown in the photograph. Join the completed front and back panels together around three sides in the same way. Insert a pillow form and join the fourth side.

TIP: FEATURE SEAMS

The panels of the pillow are joined with single crochet to make pronounced feature seams. Alternatively, you could slip stitch them together for flatter seams.

Project 11: Pointed pixie hat

This snug hat is worked in rounds using a straightforward single crochet stitch and a marled bulky-weight yarn. The multicolored effect of the yarn adds depth to the fabric's appearance. The hat is topped with a thick tassel, enhancing the fun appeal of this pixie-style hat.

BASE OF HAT

Foundation ring: Using a size N (9 mm) hook, ch 45 and join with sl st to form a ring.

Round 1 (RS): Ch 1, 1 sc into every ch to end, sl st into first ch of round.

before you start

MATERIALS
Bulky-weight yarn (42% merino wool, 30% acrylic, 28% superfine alpaca; approx. 109 yds/100 m per 4 oz/100 g ball) x 2 balls (red marl)

HOOK SIZE
N (9 mm)

GAUGE
11 sts x 10 rounds = 4" (10 cm) in single crochet

FINISHED SIZE
22" (56 cm) circumference

KEY TECHNIQUES
- Foundation chains, pages 19–20
- Single crochet, page 21
- Working in rounds, page 25
- Shaping techniques, pages 26–7
- Making tassels, page 96

ABBREVIATIONS
ch—chain
dec 1—decrease 1 stitch as follows: place hook into first sc, yo and pull through, place hook into next sc, yo and pull through (3 loops on hook), yo and pull through all 3 loops on hook
RS—right side
sc—single crochet
sl st—slip stitch
st(s)—stitch(es)
yo—yarn over

New skills/making tassels

Tassels are a great way to jazz up a crochet garment. Select the color and type of yarn to suit the mood of the piece, whether it be funky or elegant.

1 Wrap some yarn around a piece of cardboard that is the length of the tassel you want to make. About 15 wraps should be enough. Thread a piece of yarn through the top of the tassel between the yarn and the cardboard. Knot tightly to secure, leaving a long end for sewing the tassel to the garment later.

2 Cut the yarn along the bottom edge of the cardboard.

3 Wrap a length of yarn around the tassel near the top, knot tightly, then repeat 1 or 2 times. Trim the tassel.

YOU CAN NEVER HAVE ENOUGH ACCESSORIES, SO WHY NOT TRY SOME OF THE

GORGEOUS DESIGNS IN THIS CHAPTER? THE MATCHING BEANIE AND MITTENS,

WITH THEIR HUMBUG BLACK-AND-WHITE STRIPES, ARE SOFT AND WARM TO

WEAR, OR MAKE A BOLDER PERSONAL STATEMENT WITH THE POINTED PIXIE

HAT TOPPED WITH A TASSEL. THE TIE BELTS IN TWO DIFFERENT DESIGNS WILL

GO PERFECTLY WITH YOUR DENIM JEANS TO MAKE A STYLISH CASUAL OUTFIT.

chapter 4

quick-and-easy hats, mittens & belts

*Each of the four
front pillow panels
comprises four
stripes of color
in a different
sequence. The
panels are then
rotated and joined
together to create
a lively fusion of
color and pattern.*

Round 2: Ch 1, 1 sc into every sc to end, sl st into first sc.

Rounds 3–12: Repeat round 2 ten times.

SHAPING THE CROWN

Round 13: Ch 1, *1 sc into next 7 sc, dec 1, repeat from * 4 times, sl st into first sc (40 sts).

Round 14: Ch 1, 1 sc into every sc to end, sl st into first sc.

Round 15: Repeat round 14.

Round 16: Ch 1, *1 sc into next 6 sc, dec 1, repeat from * 4 times, sl st into first sc (35 sts).

Round 17: Ch 1, 1 sc into every sc to end, sl st into first sc.

Round 18: Repeat round 17.

Round 19: Ch 1, *1 sc into next 5 sc, dec 1, repeat from * 4 times, sl st into first sc (30 sts)

Round 20: Repeat round 17.

Round 21: Ch 1, *1 sc into next 4 sc, dec 1, repeat from * 4 times, sl st into first sc (25 sts).

Round 22: Repeat round 17.

Round 23: Ch 1, *1 sc into next 3 sc, dec 1, repeat from * 4 times, sl st into first sc (20 sts).

Round 24: Repeat round 17.

Round 25: Ch 1, *1 sc into next 2 sc, dec 1, repeat from * 4 times, sl st into first sc (15 sts).

Round 26: Repeat round 17.

Round 27: Ch 1, *1 sc into next sc, dec 1, repeat from * 4 times, sl st into first sc (10 sts).

Round 28: Ch 1, (dec 1) 5 times (5 sts).

Round 29: Yo and draw through all loops on hook.
Fasten off yarn.

FINISHING

Weave in any loose ends, then block and press the hat into shape. Make a tassel and sew it to the top point of the hat.

Choose a richly colored yarn to accentuate the warm and cozy appeal of this hat. With a jaunty tassel dangling from the cute pixie point, it will brighten up the coldest of winter days.

Project 12: Striped beanie

This striped hat is very easy to make. Worked in rounds from the bottom up, there are not even any seams to sew. Creating the stripe pattern is simple to do and seems to make your work grow faster.

BASE OF HAT

Foundation ring: Using a size N (9 mm) hook and yarn A, ch 45 and join with sl st to form a ring.

Round 1 (RS): Ch 1, 1 sc into every ch to end, sl st into first ch of round.

Round 2: Ch 1, 1 sc into every sc to end, sl st into first sc.

Round 3: Repeat round 2.

Rounds 4–5: Change to yarn B and repeat round 2.

Rounds 6–12: Repeat round 2, maintaining the correct stripe sequence—that is, work 3 rounds in yarn A and then 2 rounds in yarn B throughout pattern.

If you want to make the hat deeper, do so now before decreasing to shape the crown. Remember to maintain the stripe sequence.

SHAPING THE CROWN

Shape the crown as follows, maintaining the 3 rounds yarn A, 2 rounds yarn B stripe sequence throughout.

Round 1 (RS): Ch 1, (1 sc into next 7 sc, dec 1) 5 times, sl st into first sc (40 sts).

Round 2: Ch 1, 1 sc into every sc to end.

Round 3: Ch 1, (1 sc into next 6 sc, dec 1) 5 times, sl st into first sc (35 sts).

Round 4: Repeat round 2.

Round 5: Ch 1, (1 sc into next 5 sc, dec 1) 5 times, sl st into first sc (30 sts).

Round 6: Repeat round 2.

Round 7: Ch 1, (1 sc into next 4 sc, dec 1) 5 times, sl st into first sc (25 sts).

Round 8: Ch 1, (1 sc into next 3 sc, dec 1) 5 times, sl st into first sc (20 sts).

Round 9: Ch 1, (1 sc into next 2 sc, dec 1) 5 times, sl st into first sc (15 sts).

Round 10: Ch 1, (1 sc into next sc, dec 1) 5 times, sl st into first sc (10 sts).

Round 11: Ch 1, (dec 1) 5 times, sl st into first sc (5 sts).

Round 12: Ch 1, *place hook into next sc, yo and pull through, repeat from * until 5 loops remain on hook, yo and pull through all 5 loops on hook.
Fasten off yarn.

FINISHING

Weave in any loose ends.

before you start

MATERIALS
Bulky-weight yarn (100% pure new wool; approx. 109 yds/100 m per 4 oz/100 g ball) in 2 colors:
A Ecru x 1 ball
B Black x 1 ball

HOOK SIZE
N (9 mm)

GAUGE
9 sts x 10 rows = 4" (10 cm) in single crochet

FINISHED SIZE
20" (51 cm) circumference

KEY TECHNIQUES
• Foundation chains, pages 19–20
• Single crochet, page 21
• Joining a new color, page 24
• Working in rounds, page 25
• Shaping techniques, pages 26–7

ABBREVIATIONS
ch—chain
dec 1—decrease 1 stitch as follows: place hook into first sc, yo and pull through, place hook into next sc, yo and pull through (3 loops on hook), yo and pull through all 3 loops on hook
RS—right side
sc—single crochet
sl st—slip stitch
st(s)—stitch(es)
yo—yarn over

Striking stripes of black and white make this simple design stand out from the crowd. You can also make a pair of matching mittens to complement the beanie (see pages 70–1).

Project 13: Striped mittens

These mittens are crocheted in a bulky-weight wool yarn in a two-tone stripe pattern. The hand section is worked as a flat piece, while the thumb is worked in the round and then sewn into position. The mittens are crocheted using a smaller hook than usual for this weight of yarn in order to create a compact fabric that will keep the cold out and the warmth in, perfect for chilly winter days.

before you start

MATERIALS

Bulky-weight yarn (100% pure new wool; approx. 109 yds/100 m per 4 oz/100 g ball) in 2 colors:

A Ecru x 1 ball

B Black x 1 ball

HOOK SIZE

J (6 mm)

GAUGE

11 sts x 12 rows = 4" (10 cm) in single crochet

FINISHED SIZE

To fit average adult hand

KEY TECHNIQUES

- Foundation chains, pages 19–20
- Single crochet, page 21
- Joining a new color, page 24
- Working in rounds, page 25
- Shaping techniques, pages 26–7
- Seams, pages 33–4

ABBREVIATIONS

ch—chain

dec—decrease each of specified number of stitches as follows: place hook into first sc, yo and pull through, place hook into next sc, yo and pull through (3 loops on hook), yo and pull through all 3 loops on hook

RS—right side

sc—single crochet

sl st—slip stitch

st(s)—stitch(es)

yo—yarn over

HANDS (MAKE 2)

Foundation row: Using a size J (6 mm) hook and yarn A, ch 20.

Row 1 (RS): Ch 1, 1 sc into 2nd ch from hook, 1 sc into every ch to end.

Row 2: Ch 1, 1 sc into every sc to end.

Row 3: Repeat row 2.

Rows 4–5: Change to yarn B and repeat row 2.

Rows 6–18: Repeat row 2, maintaining the correct stripe sequence—that is, work 3 rows in yarn A and then 2 rows in yarn B.

Change to yarn B and start decreasing.

Row 19: Ch 1, dec 1, 6 sc, dec 2, 6 sc, dec 1 (16 sts).

Row 20: Ch 1, 1 sc into every sc to end. Change to yarn A.

Row 21: Ch 1, dec 1, 4 sc, dec 2, 4 sc, dec 1 (12 sts).

Row 22: Repeat row 20.

Row 23: Ch 1, dec 1, 2 sc, dec 2, 2 sc, dec 1 (8 sts).

Fasten off yarn.

THUMBS (MAKE 2)

Start at top of thumb.

Foundation ring: Using a size J (6 mm) hook and yarn A, ch 4 and join with sl st to form a ring.

Round 1 (RS): Ch 1, 8 sc into ring, sl st into first ch of round (9 sts).

Round 2: Ch 1, 1 sc into every sc to end, sl st into first sc.

Rounds 3–7: Repeat round 2. Fasten off yarn.

FINISHING

Weave in any loose ends, then block and press the pieces. With right sides together and starting from the wrist, backstitch the side seam until you reach the start of the 10th row from the foundation chain. Position the thumb and sew into position, then sew the rest of the side seam.

CORD

Using a size J (6 mm) hook and yarn A, ch 120. Fasten off yarn. Attach the ends of the cord to the foundation chains on the mittens on the opposite side to the thumbs.

These thick woolen mittens are attached to a long cord that runs through the inside of your coat sleeves. This handy device means that you can easily pop the mittens on and off whenever you need to without the risk of losing them.

Project 14: Mock cable tie belt

This urban chic textured tie belt has been worked using a cotton denim yarn in a natural shade. The mock cable stitch combined with the crisp utilitarian quality of the yarn help to lend weight and substance to the design, allowing the belt to keep its shape and sit perfectly on the hips.

CROCHETING THE BELT

Foundation chain: Using a size E (3.5 mm) hook, ch 14.

Row 1 (RS): Ch 1, 1 sc into 2nd ch from hook, 1 sc into every ch to end.

Row 2: Ch 3, skip 1 sc, *1 dc into next 3 sc, mcs, repeat from * to last ch, 1 dc.

Row 3: Ch 1, 1 sc into every dc, ending 1 sc into 3rd ch of ch 3.

Rows 2–3 form the mock cable stitch pattern.

Rows 4–165: Repeat rows 2–3 until 81 mock cable stitch patterns have been worked, ending with a sc row.

The belt can be increased or reduced in length simply by altering the number of pattern repeat rows worked. If you want to alter the width, either increase or reduce the number the cable stitch pattern repeats within the rows. Remember that this will alter the quantity of yarn needed.

before you start

MATERIALS

DK-weight yarn (100% cotton denim; approx. 100 yds/93 m per 2 oz/50 g ball) x 2 balls (ecru)

HOOK SIZE

E (3.5 mm)

GAUGE

1 mock cable stitch pattern = ¾" (2 cm)

FINISHED SIZE

2½ x 60" (6 x 152 cm)

KEY TECHNIQUES

- Foundation chains, pages 19–20
- Single crochet, page 21
- Double crochet, pages 22–3

ABBREVIATIONS

ch—chain

dc—double crochet

mcs—work mock cable stitch as follows: 1 dc into last skipped sc

RS—right side

sc—single crochet

TIP: STRIPE IT

The belt is worked in a continuous strip, repeating the two rows of mock cable stitch until the required length is achieved. Alternatively, it can be worked in stripes of different colors to add an extra dimension to the cable texture.

Worn slung low
on the hips, this
attractive belt will
complement any
casual outfit
and will look
especially good
with your favorite
pair of jeans.

Project 15: Denim square tie belt

This is an easy project to make and can be completed over a couple of evenings. Each square motif is worked individually and then joined with the others in a continuous strip. The cotton denim yarn gives a modern twist to this traditional pattern, and will wash well and become attractively faded with age, just like your favorite pair of jeans. Use different shades of denim for each round, as here, or work each square in a solid shade and alternate the colors as you go.

before you start

MATERIALS

DK-weight yarn (100% cotton denim; approx. 100 yds/93 m per 2 oz/50 g ball) in 3 colors:

A Ecru x 1 ball
B Blue x 1 ball
C Navy x 1 ball

HOOK SIZE

E (3.5 mm)

GAUGE

1 square motif = 3" (7 cm)

FINISHED SIZE

2½ x 60" (6 x 152 cm)

KEY TECHNIQUES

- Foundation chains, pages 19–20
- Double crochet, pages 22–3
- Joining a new color, page 24
- Working in rounds, page 25
- Seams, pages 33–4

ABBREVIATIONS

ch—chain
dc—double crochet
RS—right side
sl st—slip stitch
st(s)—stitch(es)

SQUARE MOTIFS (MAKE 20)

Foundation ring: Using a size E (3.5 mm) hook and yarn A, ch 6 and join with sl st to form a ring.

Round 1 (RS): Ch 6, *3 dc into ring, ch 3, repeat from * twice, 2 dc into ring, sl st into 3rd ch of ch 6.
Change to yarn B and join to any ch 3 space.

Round 2: Ch 6, 3 dc into next ch space, *ch 1, 3 dc into next ch space, ch 3, 3 dc into same ch space, repeat from * twice, ch 1, 2 dc into next ch space, sl st into 3rd ch of ch 6.
Change to yarn C and join to any ch 3 corner space.

Round 3: Ch 6, 3 dc into next ch space, *(ch 1, 3 dc into next ch space) twice, ch 3, 3 dc into same ch space, repeat from * twice, (ch 1, 3 dc into next ch space) twice, ch 3, 2 dc into same ch space, sl st into 3rd ch of ch 6. Fasten off yarn.

FINISHING

Weave in any loose ends. Wash all the square motifs in a washing machine set to a hot cycle; this will remove surface dye from the denim yarn and create a faded effect. Along with squares, wash enough of yarn C to sew all the motifs together. With right sides facing, sew the squares together in a strip using a woven seam.

TIP: CHANGE THE LENGTH

The length of the belt can be easily altered by increasing or reducing the number of square motifs. Remember that if you lengthen the belt, more yarn may be needed.

Remember that some of the dye will come out of cotton denim yarn when you wash it, so take care what you put in the washing machine with this belt until you are sure that the fading process is complete.

quick-and-easy wraps & garments

THESE WRAPS AND GARMENTS ARE ESSENTIAL ITEMS FOR EVERY WOMAN'S

WARDROBE. THE TRADITIONAL PICOT-MESH WRAP AND MODERN OPEN-MESH

SHRUG ARE PERFECT FOR DAYTIME OUTFITS, WHILE EVENING WEAR WILL BE

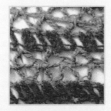

COMPLEMENTED BY THE DELICATE FABRIC OF THE BEADED WRAP AND THE

LACE EVENING WRAP. THE VERSATILE LACY CAPE CAN BE WORN BOTH DAY AND

NIGHT, WHILE THE STRIPED PONCHO MAKES A FUNKIER FASHION STATEMENT.

Project 16: Lacy cape

This beautifully simple cape should be an essential piece in any woman's wardrobe. Worked in a merino and alpaca wool blend, it is perfect for throwing over your shoulders on chilly spring and fall days.

CAPE PANEL

Foundation chain: Using a size P (10 mm) hook, ch 36.

Row 1 (RS): Ch 2, 1 dc into 3rd ch from hook, 1 dc into every ch to end.

Row 2: Ch 2, 1 dc into every dc to end.

Row 3: Ch 2, 1 dc into first dc, *2 dc into next dc, 1 dc, repeat from * to end (54 sts).

Row 4: Repeat row 2.

Row 5: Ch 2, 2 dc, *2 dc into next dc, 2 dc, repeat from * to end (72 sts).

Row 6: Repeat row 2.

Row 7: Ch 2, 3 dc, *2 dc into next dc, 3 dc, repeat from * to end (90 sts).

Row 8: Repeat row 2.

Row 9: Ch 2, 4 dc, *2 dc into next dc, 4 dc, repeat from * to end (108 sts).

Rows 10–11: Repeat row 2.

Fasten off yarn.

PICOT TRIM

Using a size L (8 mm) hook and with right side facing, join yarn at top left corner. Work picot trim as follows: *2 sc into sc of neck edge, ch 3, 1 sc into same space as last of previous 2 sc, repeat from * to end around whole edge of cape (94 picots).

FINISHING

Weave in any loose ends, then block and press to the correct size. Sew the button into position at the neck edge on the left side of the cape. Use the picot trim at the opposite side of the cape as a fastening loop.

before you start

MATERIALS

Bulky-weight yarn (42% merino wool, 30% acrylic, 28% superfine alpaca; approx. 109 yds/100 m per 4 oz/100 g ball) x 3 balls (beige)
1 large shell button

HOOK SIZE

L (8 mm), P (10 mm)

GAUGE

6 sts x 5 rows = 4" (10 cm) in pattern

FINISHED SIZE

10" (25 cm) deep with picot trim x 61" (155 cm) wide at lower edge

KEY TECHNIQUES

• Foundation chains, pages 19–20
• Double crochet, pages 22–3

ABBREVIATIONS

ch—chain
dc—double crochet
RS—right side
st(s)—stitch(es)

The choice of a neutral color yarn allows the lace work to be the main attraction of this cape, and has the added bonus that the cape will complement many different outfits.

Project 17: Picot-mesh wrap

Worked in two separate pieces, this beautiful wrap uses a super bulky-weight merino yarn in a simple picot mesh stitch. Quick to crochet, it is also light and cozy to wear. The border trim adds structure to the finished piece and helps define the wrap's versatile shape.

before you start

MATERIALS

A Super bulky-weight yarn (100% merino wool; approx. 87 yds/ 80 m per 4 oz/100 g ball) x 5 balls (light cream)
B Bulky-weight yarn (100% pure new wool; approx. 109 yds/100 m per 4 oz/100 g ball) x 1 ball (dark cream)

HOOK SIZE

J (6 mm), N (9 mm)

GAUGE

Swatch = ch 12 and work five rows; 2 repeats of pattern (5 sts + 3 for picot) x 4 rows = 10 cm (4")

FINISHED SIZE

16" (40 cm) wide x 40" (100 cm) long

TECHNIQUES USED

• Foundation chains, page 19–20
• Single crochet, page 21
• Seams, pages 33–4

ABBREVIATIONS

ch—chain
sc—single crochet
sl st—slip stitch
st(s)—stitch(es)

TIP: USING COLORED MARKERS
When placing markers for borders, use a different color for increasing and decreasing. There is only one decrease in this pattern, so the color difference should help to remind you.

SHORTER PANEL

Foundation chain: Using a size N (9 mm) hook and yarn A, ch 32.

Row 1 (RS): Ch 4, 1 sc into 8th ch from hook, (ch 3, sl st into sc just worked) to form picot, *ch 5, skip ch 3, 1 sc into next ch, ch 3, sl st into sc just worked, repeat from *, ending with 1 sc into last ch.

Row 2: Ch 5, skip first sc, *1 sc into ch 5 space, ch 3, sl st into sc just worked, ch 5, skip next sc and picot, repeat from *, ending with 1 sc in 3rd ch of ch 7. Row 2 forms the pattern. Repeat row 2 another 28 times until the panel measures 30" (75 cm) or the required length is achieved.

Next row: *Ch 3, 1 sc into 3rd ch of ch 5, repeat from * to end. Fasten off yarn.

LONGER PANEL

Work as instructed for the shorter panel until it measures 40" (100 cm) long (approx. 40 repeats in total) or the required length is achieved.

SEWING UP

Weave in any loose ends, then block and press the pieces to the correct size. Butt a short edge of the shorter panel up to one end of a long edge of the longer panel to create a V shape (the point forms the back of the wrap) and sew together with a woven seam.

BORDER TRIM

With a size J (6 mm) hook and yarn B, and with right side facing, edge the cape with single crochet. Join the final sc to the first sc with a sl st. Place a marker at every corner. Work a second row of sc around the cape, working 3 sc into 1 sc at the outer corners (increase) and decreasing by skipping 2 sc at the inner corner. Fasten off yarn.

Two different yarns in similar colors are used here, but you can easily add a new dimension to this design by playing with the color combinations.

Project 18: Lace evening wrap

Light and lacy motifs are worked in a luxurious silk yarn to make this delightful evening wrap. The lace motifs are joined together as you go and the outside of the wrap is trimmed with a neat edging.

Motif A

Foundation ring: Using a size C (3 mm) hook, ch 7 and join with sl st to form a ring.

Round 1 (RS): Ch 3, *ch 2, 1 dc into ring, repeat from * ten times, ch 2, join with sl st to 3rd ch of ch 3 (12 spaced dc).

Round 2: Ch 3, *ch 3, 1 dc into next dc, repeat from * ten times, ch 3, join with sl st to 3rd ch of ch 3 (12 spaced dc).

Round 3: *Into next ch 3 space work 1 sc, 1 hdc, 1 dc, 1 hdc, 1 sc (1 shell made), repeat from * eleven times, join with sl st into first sc (12 shells).

Round 4: Sl st across next hdc and into dc at top of shell, *ch 7, 1 sc into dc at center of next shell, repeat from * ten times, ch 7, join with sl st into first ch of ch 7 (12 spaces).

Round 5: *Into next space work 4 sc, ch 11, 4 sc to form corner, into each of next 2 spaces work 4 sc, ch 3 (to form picot), 4 sc, repeat from * three times, join with sl st to first sc.

Fasten off yarn.

Motif B

Work as instructed for motif A until round 4 has been completed, then join one side of motif B to one side of motif A as follows:

Round 5: Work as round 5 of motif A for the first 3 spaces, into 4th space work 4 sc, ch 5, place WS of both motifs together, and join by working 1 sc into ch 11 corner space of motif A, ch 5, return to 4th space of motif B, work another 4 sc to complete corner, *into next space work 4 sc, ch 1, 1 sc into corresponding picot of motif A, ch 1, 4 sc into same space of motif B, repeat from * once, then into next corner space of motif B work 4 sc, ch 5, 1 sc into ch 11 corner space of motif A, ch 5, another 4 sc into same space of motif B to complete corner, work remainder of motif as instructed for motif A.

Fasten off yarn.

Motifs C, D, E, F, G

Working in this way, join four more motifs (C, D, E, F) to A and B to make a strip of six joined motifs.

Work the top motif of the second strip (G) in the same way as motif B, joining it to the side edge of motif A.

Motif H

Round 5 (to work spaces 1, 2, 3): Work as round 5 of motif A for the first 3 spaces.

Round 5 (to join spaces 4, 5, 6): Into 4th space work 4 sc, ch 5, place WS of motifs G and H together and join by working 1 sc into ch 11 corner space of motif G, ch 5, return to 4th space of motif H, work another 4 sc to complete corner, *into next space work 4 sc, ch 1, 1 sc into corresponding picot of motif G, ch 1, 4 sc into same space of motif H, repeat from * once.

Round 5 (to join spaces 7, 8, 9): Into next corner space of motif H work 4 sc, ch 5, 1 sc into ch 11 corner space of motif G, ch 5, work another 4 sc into same space

before you start

MATERIALS
Sport-weight yarn (100% silk; approx. 210 yds/192 m per 2 oz/50 g ball) x 8 balls (pink)

HOOK SIZE
C (3 mm)

GAUGE
One motif = 4" (10 cm) from picot to picot

FINISHED SIZE
6 x 18 motifs = 24 x 72" (61 x 183 cm)

KEY TECHNIQUES
- Foundation chains, pages 19–20
- Single crochet, page 21
- Double crochet, pages 22–3
- Half double crochet, page 23
- Working in rounds, page 25
- Lace work, pages 28–9

ABBREVIATIONS
ch—chain
dc—double crochet
hdc—half double crochet
RS—right side
sc—single crochet
sl st—slip stitch
st(s)—stitch(es)
WS—wrong side

of motif H to complete corner, place WS of motifs B and H together, *into next space of motif H work 4 sc, ch 1, 1 sc into corresponding picot of motif B, ch 1, 4 sc into same space of motif H, repeat from * once.

Round 5 (to work spaces 10, 11, 12): Into next corner space of motif H work 4 sc, ch 5, 1 sc into ch 11 corner space of motif B, ch 5, work another 4 sc into same space of motif H to complete corner. Work remainder of motif as instructed for motif A.

Fasten off yarn.

COMPLETING THE MOTIFS

Working in this way, join 4 more motifs (I, J, K, L) together to complete the second strip. Continue adding strips of six motifs, starting at the top of each strip and working in the same way until you have 18 strips of motifs joined together.

BORDER TRIM

With right side of the wrap facing, join the yarn to the first ch 3 space on the top long edge.

Round 1 (RS): Ch 1, 1 sc into same space, *ch 6, 1 sc into next ch 3 space, ch 9, 1 sc where ch 11 spaces meet, ch 9, 1 sc into next ch 3 space, repeat from * to end, working (ch 9, 1 sc into ch 11 space, ch 9) into single ch 11 space at each corner, join with sl st to first sc.

Round 2: Ch 1, *6 sc into ch 6 space, 1 sc into next sc, 9 sc into ch 9 space, 1 sc into next sc twice, repeat from * to end, working 3 sc into sc at each corner, join with sl st into first ch.

Fasten off yarn.

FINISHING

Weave in any loose ends. Working in sections, block the wrap and spray the pinned section lightly with cold water. Allow each section to dry thoroughly before removing the pins and moving onto the next section.

The silk yarn used for this project is beautiful but expensive. For a cheaper alternative, try a cotton or synthetic yarn to make a less luxurious but equally pretty wrap.

Project 19: Open-mesh shrug

This modern alternative to a cardigan, made up of two simple tubes joined together across the back, is extremely versatile—you can wear it with your arms in the sleeves or simply wrap the shrug around your neck as a scarf. Worked in a bulky-weight yarn and an open-mesh stitch, it is both light and cozy.

SLEEVE TUBES (MAKE 2)

Foundation ring: Using a size N (9 mm) hook, ch 36 and join with sl st to form a ring.

Round 1 (RS): Ch 1, 1 sc into every ch to end, sl st into first ch.

Round 2: Ch 5, skip 1 sc, *1 tr, ch 1, skip 1 sc, repeat from * to end, sl st into 3rd ch of ch 5.

Round 3: Ch 5, *1 tr into next tr, ch 1, repeat from * to end, sl st into 3rd ch of ch 5.

Repeat round 3 until sleeve measures approximately 23" (59 cm) long.

ARMHOLE SHAPING

Row 1: *Sl st into first ch, sl st into next tr, repeat from * three times, ch 5, skip (ch 1, 1 tr, ch 1), 1 tr into next tr, **ch 1, skip ch 1, 1 tr into next tr, repeat from ** ten times, ch 1, skip (ch 1, 1 tr), 1 tr into next ch, turn.

Row 2: Ch 5, skip (ch 1, 1 tr, ch 1), *1 tr into next tr, ch 1, skip ch 1, repeat from * six times, skip (ch 1, 1 tr, ch 1), 1 tr into next tr, turn.

Row 3: Ch 5, skip ch 1, *ch 1, 1 tr into next tr, repeat from * to end, turn.
Repeat row 3 four more times.
Fasten off yarn.

SEWING UP

Weave in any loose ends. With right sides together, backstitch the two sleeves together across the top of the armhole shaping.

BORDER TRIM

Using a size J (6.5 mm) hook, join yarn at base of center seam with right side facing.

Row 1: Ch 1, then evenly space approximately 148 sc around outer edge. Join together with a sl st into first ch.

Row 2: Ch 1, 1 sc into next 33 sc, (1 sc, skip 2 sc) 26 times, 1 dc into every dc to end, join together with a sl st into first ch.
Fasten off yarn.

This contemporary fashion item is the perfect answer for those days that are too warm for a cardigan or sweater but not warm enough to go without any arm covering.

Project 20: Beaded wrap

This stylish wrap is a useful piece for day or evening wear. It is crocheted in a wonderfully soft kid mohair and silk blend yarn to produce a light, delicate fabric. Beads placed throughout the fabric add to the tactile surface to create a simply must-have piece.

before you start

MATERIALS

Fingering-weight yarn (70% super kid mohair, 30% silk; approx. 229 yds/210 m per 1 oz/25 g ball) x 3 balls (cream)
Approx. 4,000 small silver beads

HOOK SIZE

E (3.5 mm)

GAUGE

Not important, but change to a larger hook if you feel it is too tight

FINISHED SIZE

16 x 60" (40 x 150 cm)

KEY TECHNIQUES

- Foundation chains, pages 19–20
- Single crochet, page 21
- Incorporating beads, page 88

ABBREVIATIONS

bsc—beaded single crochet
ch—chain
RS—right side
sc—single crochet
st(s)—stitch(es)

CROCHETING THE WRAP

The quantity of beads required for this design is too much to thread onto the yarn in one go, so thread them approximately 200 at a time. Break off the yarn when all 200 beads have been used, then thread another 200 beads onto the yarn. Repeat until complete.

Foundation chain: Using a size E (3.5 mm) hook, ch 120.

Row 1 (RS): 1 sc into 10th ch from hook, *ch 5, skip ch 4, 1 bsc into next ch, repeat from * to end.

Row 2: *Ch 6, 1 bsc into next ch 5 space, repeat from * to end.

Repeat row 2 until required length is achieved. Fasten off yarn.

FINISHING

Weave in any loose ends.

The fine yarn
and lacy stitch
pattern combine
to create a
luxurious cobweb
of fabric that is
perfectly enhanced
by the sparkling
silver beads.

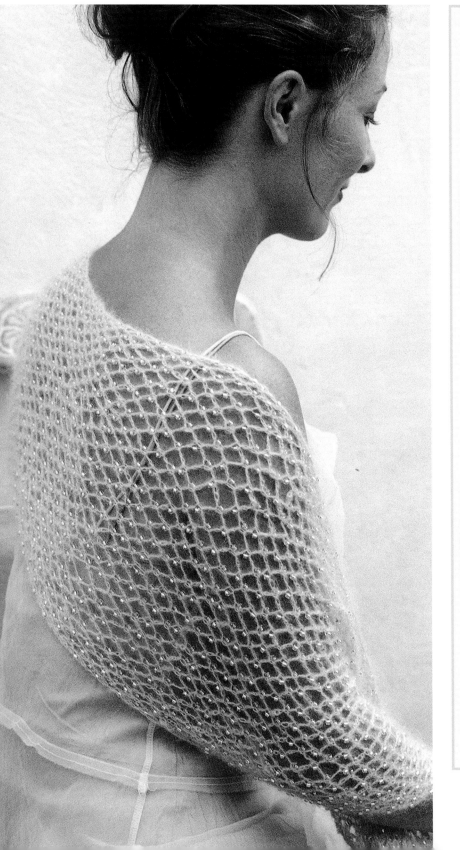

New skills/ incorporating beads and sequins

It is easy to incorporate beads and sequins into crochet fabrics. Any type of beads and sequins can be used, provided that the central hole is large enough for the yarn to pass through.

1 Thread a sewing needle with a short length of sewing cotton and knot the ends. Pass the yarn through the loop made. Slide each bead or sequin onto the needle, then down the sewing cotton and onto the yarn. Pull the yarn through and continue threading on beads or sequins in this way.

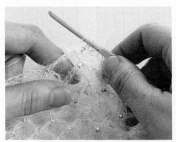

2 When indicated in the pattern, push a bead or sequin up the yarn to sit just below the crochet hook. Work the next stitch as instructed— in this case, single crochet—leaving the bead or sequin at the front of the work.

Project 21: Striped poncho

This 1970s-style poncho has been updated through the use of color and stitch pattern. The poncho is edged with a fringe of brightly colored tassels, but you could try using different types of trims instead. Crocheted from the top down, you will see results fast.

CROCHETING THE PONCHO

The pattern starts at the neck edge of the poncho.

Foundation chain: Using a size J (6 mm) hook and yarn A, ch 58.

Row 1: Ch 1, 1 sc into 2nd ch from hook, 1 sc into every ch to end.

Row 2: Ch 3, 1 tr into every sc to end. Change to yarn B.

Row 3: Ch 3, (skip 1 st, 1 tr into next st) twice, *ch 2, C2, repeat from * to last 3 sts (including ch), ch 1, 1 tr into st just worked, skip 1 st, 1 tr into next st, 1 tr into 3rd ch of ch 3.

Row 4: Ch 3, skip 1 st, 1 tr into next st, ch 1, *C2, ch 2, repeat from * to last 5 sts, C2, ch 1, 1 tr into next st, 1 tr into 3rd ch of ch 3.

before you start

MATERIALS

Aran-weight yarn (70% lambswool, 26% kid mohair, 4% nylon; (approx. 153 yds/140 m per 2 oz/50 g ball) in 2 colors:

A Red x 3 balls

B Orange x 3 balls

C Extra super bulky-weight yarn (100% merino wool; approx. 33 yds/30 m per 4 oz/100 g ball) x 2 balls (pink)

1 large shell button

HOOK SIZE

J (6 mm)

GAUGE

16 sts x 6 rows = 4" (10 cm) in pattern

FINISHED SIZE

16" (40 cm) long at side seam

20" (50 cm) long at center point

KEY TECHNIQUES

• Foundation chains, pages 19–20
• Single crochet, page 21
• Treble crochet, page 24
• Seams, pages 33–4
• Tassel fringe, page 52

ABBREVIATIONS

C2—yo twice, draw loop through st just worked, (yo, draw loop through first 2 loops on hook) twice, skip 2 sts, yo twice, draw loop through next st, (yo, draw loop through first 2 loops on hook) twice, yo, draw loop through remaining 3 loops

ch—chain

RS—right side

sc—single crochet

st(s)—stitch(es)

tr—treble crochet

yo—yarn over

TIP: TASSEL VARIATIONS
The tassels are a great way of adding your own character to the poncho. This example uses a contrasting colored thicker yarn, but many options are possible. Try using more strands of a finer yarn and thread beads onto the ends for a glamorous touch.

Change to yarn A.

Row 5: Ch 3, skip 1 st, 1 tr into next 23 sts, 2 tr into next st, 3 tr into next 8 sts, 2 tr into next st, 1 tr into every st to end, 1 tr into top of ch 3 (76 sts).
Continue changing color as set in the previous rows.

Rows 6–7: Repeat rows 3–4.

Row 8: Ch 3, skip 1 st, 1 tr into next 32 sts, 2 tr into next st, 3 tr into next 8 sts, 2 tr into next st, 1 tr into every st to end, 1 tr into top of ch 3 (94 sts).

Rows 9–10: Repeat rows 3–4.

Row 11: Ch 3, skip 1 st, 1 tr into next 41 sts, 2 tr into next st, 3 tr into next 8 sts, 2 tr into next st, 1 tr into every st to end, 1 tr into top of ch 3 (112 sts).

Rows 12–13: Repeat rows 3–4.

Row 14: Ch 3, skip 1 st, 1 tr into next 50 sts, 2 tr into next st, 3 tr into next 8 sts, 2 tr into next st, 1 tr into each st to end, 1 tr into top of ch 3 (130 sts).

Rows 15–16: Repeat rows 3–4.

Row 17: Ch 3, skip 1 st, 1 tr into next 59 sts, 2 tr into next sts, 3 tr into next 8 sts, 2 tr into next st, 1 tr into every st to end, 1 tr into top of ch 3 (148 sts).

Row 18: 1 sc into every st to end, 1 sc into top of ch 3.
Fasten off yarn.

FINISHING

Weave in any loose ends, then block and press to the correct size. With right sides together, backstitch the edges of the poncho together, leaving the first six rows unsewn for the neck opening. Attach a button to the top of the neck opening on one side of the poncho. Work a chain at the opposite side and join the other end of the chain to the poncho to form a button loop. Cut 12" (30 cm) lengths of yarn C and add a tassel fringe around the edges.

The colorful stripe design of the poncho is accentuated by the contrasting shapes of the stitch patterns.

quick-and-easy scarves

KEEPING YOURSELF COZY HAS NEVER BEEN SO MUCH FUN. FROM THE QUIRKY

BOBBLES ON A STRING TO THE COZY FELTED SCARF AND CUDDLY POMPON-

TRIMMED SCARF, YOU WILL FIND SOMETHING SUITABLE FOR EVERY SEASON.

THE SEQUINNED SCARF AND CHEVRON-STRIPED SCARF ARE THE PERFECT

PIECES TO CARRY YOU THROUGH FROM DAY TO EVENING. THE SKINNY BEADED

SCARF HAS A YOUNG AND MODERN APPEAL, AND IS VERSATILE TO WEAR.

Project 22: Bobbles on a string

This scarf updates the traditional pompon idea by layering different-sized crocheted flowers together to form the bobbles and threading them onto a crocheted chain. Quick to make and quirky to wear, this project is perfect for using up leftover scraps of yarn.

SMALL FLOWER (MAKE 24)

Foundation ring: Using a size F (4 mm) hook and yarn B, ch 6 and join with sl st to form a ring.

Round 1: Ch 1, 15 sc into center of ring, sl st into first ch.

Round 2: *Ch 10, skip 1 sc, sl st into next sc, repeat from * , ending with sl st into first ch of ch 10.

Fasten off yarn.

MEDIUM FLOWER (MAKE 24)

Using a size H (5 mm) hook and yarn C, work as instructed for the small flower.

LARGE FLOWER (MAKE 12)

Using a size J (6 mm) hook and yarn D, work as instructed for the small flower.

CENTER CORD

Using a size N (9 mm) hook and yarn A, make a 64" (160 cm) long foundation chain. Fasten off yarn.

FINISHING

Weave in any loose ends. To make each bobble, layer the flowers in the following order: 1 small, 1 medium, 1 large, 1 medium, 1 small. Sew them together through their central rings using yarn B. Tie a large double knot at one end of the cord and thread on the first bobble. Tie another knot at the other side of the bobble to hold it in place. Thread on the remaining bobbles, tying a knot on each side to hold them in place, and ensuring that they are evenly spaced along the cord.

TIP: BOBBLE VARIATIONS

The flowers that make up the bobbles in this project can be worked in any thickness of yarn, so why not try some of your own combinations to produce bigger or more delicate bobbles. Alternatively, you could felt the flowers in a washing machine (see page 41). Remember that felting only works if you are using 100 percent wool yarn and can drastically alter the finished size, so more yarn may be needed.

before you start

MATERIALS

A Extra super bulky-weight yarn (100% merino wool; approx. 33 yds/30 m per 4 oz/100 g ball) x 1 ball (black)

B DK-weight yarn (100% pure new wool; approx. 124 yds/113 m per 2 oz/50 g ball) x 1 ball (purple)

C Aran-weight yarn (100% pure new wool; approx. 175 yds/160 m per 4 oz/100 g ball) x 1 ball (blue)

D Bulky-weight yarn (100% pure new wool; approx. 109 yds/100 m per 4 oz/100 g ball) x 1 ball (khaki)

HOOK SIZE

F (4 mm), H (5 mm), J (6 mm), N (9 mm)

GAUGE

Not important

FINISHED SIZE

Approx. 60" (150 cm) long

KEY TECHNIQUES

• Foundation chains, pages 19–20
• Working in rounds, page 25
• Single crochet, page 21

ABBREVIATIONS

ch—chain
sc—single crochet
sl st—slip stitch
st(s)—stitch(es)

If you do not have sufficient yarn to make this scarf, reduce the length of the central cord and use fewer bobbles —a string of bobbles just half this length would also look great.

Project 23: Sequinned scarf

This delicate sequinned scarf is worked mainly in a double crochet net fabric that is enhanced by the soft kid mohair and silk blend yarn. The ends are finished with a sequinned single crochet stitch, giving the scarf an elegant evening twist.

before you start

MATERIALS

Fingering-weight yarn (70% super kid mohair, 30% silk; approx. 229 yds/210 m per 1 oz/25 g ball) x 2 balls (green)
Approx. 300 iridescent sequins

HOOK SIZE

F (4 mm)

GAUGE

10 sts x 8 rows = 4" (10 cm) in double crochet net stitch

FINISHED SIZE

6 x 60" (15 x 150 cm)

KEY TECHNIQUES

- Foundation chains, pages 19–20
- Single crochet, page 21
- Double crochet, pages 22–3
- Incorporating sequins, page 88

ABBREVIATIONS

ch—chain
dc—double crochet
RS—right side
sc—single crochet
sqsc—sequin single crochet
st(s)—stitch(es)
WS—wrong side

CROCHETING THE SCARF

Thread half the sequins onto the first ball of yarn.

Foundation chain: Using a size F (4 mm) hook, ch 30.

Row 1 (RS): Ch 2, 1 sc into 3rd ch from hook, 1 sc into every ch to end.

Row 2: Ch 2, 1 sc, *1 sqsc, 1 sc, repeat from * to end.

Row 3: Ch 2, 1 sc into every sc to end.

Row 4: Ch 2, 2 sc, *1 sqsc, 1 sc, repeat from * to end.

Row 5: Repeat row 3.

Rows 2–5 create the sequin pattern.

Rows 6–22: Repeat rows 2–5 four times, then repeat row 3 once.

Change to double crochet net stitch as follows:

Row 23: Ch 3, 1 dc into first sc, *ch 1, skip 1 sc, 1 dc, repeat from * to last sc, 1 dc.

Row 24: Ch 3, 1 dc into first dc, *ch 1, 1 dc into first ch space, repeat from * to last dc, 1 dc.

Repeat row 24 until the work measures 56" (140 cm) or the required length is achieved, ending on a WS row. This is the easiest place in the pattern to make the scarf longer or shorter, so work more or fewer rows as necessary.

Next row: Ch 2, *1 sc into next dc, 1 sc into next space, repeat from * to end.

Repeat rows 2–22 to work a sequinned single crochet fabric at the end of the scarf. Fasten off yarn.

FINISHING

Weave in any loose ends.

TIP: USING BEADS

You could just as easily use beads instead of sequins, or a combination of both. Remember that the first sequin/bead you put onto the yarn will be the last one used.

Sequins are the perfect way to add a touch of glamour to an evening outfit. These iridescent sequins have an attractive sparkle but do not overpower the delicacy of the crochet fabric.

Project 24: Pompon-trimmed scarf

Although this scarf looks as if it is made using several different-colored yarns, it is in fact crocheted from a single yarn containing multiple shades from orange to pink to purple. Yarns like this also make fantastic pompons.

SQUARE MOTIF (MAKE 13)

Foundation ring: Using a size N (9 mm) hook, ch 6 and join with sl st to form a ring.

Round 1 (RS): Ch 6, *3 dc into ring, ch 3, repeat from * twice, 2 dc into ring, sl st into 3rd ch of ch 6.

Round 2: Ch 6, 3 dc into next ch space, *ch 1, 3 dc into next ch space, ch 3, 3 dc into same ch space, repeat from * twice, ch 1, 2 dc into next ch space, sl st into 3rd ch of ch 6. Fasten off yarn.

JOINING SQUARES

Weave in any loose ends. Join the square motifs together to form a strip by placing two squares together and joining them along one edge using single crochet.

POINTS (MAKE 1 AT EACH END)

Using a size N (9 mm) hook and with RS facing, 10 sc along one end of scarf.

Row 1: Ch 1, 1 sc into every sc to end.

Row 2: Ch 1, dec 1, 1 sc into every st until last 2 sts, dec 1, turn.

Repeat rows 1–2, dec 1 at beginning and end of row 2, until 2 sts remain. Fasten off yarn.

BORDER TRIM

With right side facing, join yarn at one point of scarf and work a single crochet edging all around the scarf. Join the final sc to the first sc with a sl st.

FINISHING

Weave in any loose ends. At each pointed end of the scarf, join the yarn and work a 10" (25 cm) chain. Make 2 pompons approx. 3⅛" (8 cm) in diameter and attach one to the end of each chain.

---

before you start

MATERIALS

Bulky-weight yarn (100% pure new wool; approx. 109 yds/100 m per 4 oz/100 g ball) x 3 balls (orange/purple mix)

HOOK SIZE

N (9 mm)

GAUGE

1 square motif = 4¼" (11 cm)

FINISHED SIZE

80" (205 cm) from point to point

KEY TECHNIQUES

- Foundation chains, pages 19–20
- Single crochet, page 21
- Double crochet, pages 22–3
- Working in rounds, page 25
- Shaping techniques, pages 26–7
- Seams, pages 33–4
- Pompons, page 36

ABBREVIATIONS

ch—chain

dc—double crochet

dec 1—decrease 1 stitch as follows: place hook into first sc, yo and pull through, place hook into next sc, yo and pull through (3 loops on hook), yo and pull through all 3 loops on hook

RS—right side

sc—single crochet

sl st—slip stitch

st(s)—stitch(es)

yo—yarn over

If you cannot find a multicolored yarn like the one used here, try crocheting each square motif in a different color, then use pieces of all the yarns to make the pompons.

Project 25: Chevron-striped scarf

This scarf is a good project to try once you have mastered the basic stitches and want to move onto something slightly more involved. Both increasing and decreasing techniques are used along a row to create the chevron stripes.

CROCHETING THE SCARF

Foundation chain: Using a size F (4 mm) hook and yarn A, ch 20.

Row 1 (RS): Ch 1, 1 sc into 2nd ch from hook, 1 sc into every ch to end.

Row 2: Ch 2, dec 2 as follows: *yo and insert into next sc, yo and pull through, yo and pull through 2 sts, repeat from * twice, yo and pull through all sts on hook; 6 dc, inc 4 as follows: 5 dc into same stitch; 6 dc, dec 2 as instructed at start of row, 1 dc.

Row 3: Ch 2, dec 2, 6 dc, inc 4 dc, 6 dc, dec 2, 1 dc.

Repeat row 3 until required length is achieved, maintaining stripe pattern as follows:

Rows 1–4: Yarn A.
Row 5: Yarn D.
Rows 6–7: Yarn B.
Row 8: Yarn D.
Rows 9–12: Yarn A.
Row 13: Yarn D.
Rows 14–15: Yarn C.
Row 16: Yarn D.
Rows 17–18: Yarn A.
Row 19: Yarn D.
Rows 20–21: Yarn B.
Row 22: Yarn D.
Rows 23–24: Yarn A.
Row 25: Yarn D.
Rows 26–27: Yarn C.
Row 28: Yarn D.
Rows 29–31: Yarn A.
Row 32: Yarn D.
Rows 33–34: Yarn B.
Row 35: Yarn D.
Rows 36–38: Yarn A.

Repeat rows 13–38 twice, then rows 16–1 once (that is, work rows 1–16 in reverse).

FINISHING

Using yarn D, edge the scarf with single crochet. Weave in any loose ends, then block and press to the correct size.

TIP: EXPERIMENT

The combination of cotton and lurex yarns used in this project gives the scarf a crisp look. Have fun playing about with color and yarn in this project. You can even vary the width of the chevron stripes to make the scarf uniquely your own.

before you start

MATERIALS

Medium–weight yarn (100% cotton; approx. 125 yds/115 m per 2 oz/50 g ball) in 3 colors:
A Green x 2 balls
B Lilac x 1 ball
C Beige x 1 ball
D Light-weight yarn (80% viscose, 20% polyester; approx. 104 yds/95 m per 1 oz/25 g ball) x 1 ball (blue)

HOOK SIZE

F (4 mm)

GAUGE

7 rows = 4" (10 cm) in chevron pattern

FINISHED SIZE

3½ x 60" (9 x 152 cm)

KEY TECHNIQUES

• Foundation chains, pages 19–20
• Single crochet, page 21
• Double crochet, pages 22–3
• Joining a new color, page 24
• Shaping techniques, pages 26–7

ABBREVIATIONS

ch—chain
dc—double crochet
dec—decrease
inc—increase
RS—right side
sc—single crochet
st(s)—stitch(es)
yo—yarn over

Project 26: Cozy felted scarf

This striking scarf looks complicated but is very easy to work. The picot mesh fabric is broken up by bold stripes of color, then felted to give the scarf a gorgeous softness. The small crochet flowers in complementary shades sewn onto each end are embellished with a funky bead to provide the perfect finishing touch.

before you start

MATERIALS

Aran-weight yarn (100% pure new wool; approx. 175 yds/160 m per 4 oz/100 g ball) in 2 colors:
A Ecru x 1 ball
B Black x 1 ball
C DK-weight yarn (100% pure new wool; approx. 124 yds/113 m per 2 oz/50 g ball) x 1 ball (red)
D Fingering-weight yarn (70% super kid mohair, 30% silk; approx. 229 yds/210 m per 1 oz/25 g ball) x 1 ball (pink)
Yarns C and D are used together throughout
Scraps of Aran-weight yarn for flowers (red and green used here)
2 large glass beads

HOOK SIZE

L (8 mm)

GAUGE

Exact gauge not important, but 2 repeats of pattern (5 sts + 3 for picot) x 6 rows = approx. 4" (10 cm) after felting

FINISHED SIZE

5½ x 60" (14 x 150 cm)

KEY TECHNIQUES

• Foundation chains, pages 19–20
• Single crochet, page 21
• Felting, page 41

ABBREVIATIONS

ch—chain
RS—right side
sc—single crochet
sl st—slip stitch
st(s)—stitch(es)

CROCHETING THE SCARF

Foundation chain: Using a size L (8 mm) hook and yarn A, ch 175.

Row 1 (RS): Ch 5, 1 sc into 10th ch from hook, ch 3, sl st into center of sc just worked, *ch 5, skip ch 4, 1 sc into next ch, ch 3, sl st into sc just worked, repeat from * to last ch 5, ch 5, skip ch 4, 1 sc.

Row 2: Ch 5, *1 sc into ch 5 space, ch 3, sl st into center of sc just worked, ch 5, repeat from * to last ch 5 space, ch 5, 1 sc.

Rows 3–4: Change to yarn B and repeat row 2 twice.

Rows 5–6: Change to yarn A and repeat row 2 twice.

Rows 7–8: Change to yarns C and D (work these together) and repeat row 2 twice. Fasten off yarn.

Go to foundation chain and use yarns C and D together for next row.

Next row: 1 sc into first ch space, ch 3, sl st into sc just worked, *ch 5, 1 sc into ch space, ch 3, sl st into sc just worked, repeat from * to end, only working a sc into last ch space. Repeat this row once more.

FINISHING

Weave in any loose ends. Make two medium-sized flowers (see project 22) and sew one flower to each end of the scarf. Loosely baste the ends of the scarf together using a cotton yarn. Felt the scarf, then remove the cotton yarn and allow to dry. Sew a decorative glass bead to the center of each flower.

Project 27: Skinny beaded scarf

This skinny scarf is a great way to add a personal touch to any outfit, whatever the season. The stripes of complementary shades give a tone-on-tone effect, letting the yarn textures speak for themselves. Random stripes of color and beaded tassels give the scarf a funky modern feel.

CROCHETING THE SCARF

Foundation chain: Using a size G (4.5 mm) hook and yarn A, ch 250.

Row 1 (RS): Ch 3, 1 sc into 8th ch from hook, *ch 5, skip ch 4, 1 sc into next ch, repeat from * to end.

Row 2: Ch 5, *1 sc into ch 5 space, ch 5, repeat from * to end.

Row 3: Change to yarn B and repeat row 2.

Row 4: Change to yarn D (doubled) and repeat row 2.

Row 5–7: Change to yarn C and repeat row 2 three times.
Fasten off yarn.

FINISHING

Weave in any loose ends. Cut fourteen 4" (10 cm) lengths of yarn D and add half to each end of the scarf as a tassel fringe. Thread a bead onto the end of each tassel and knot securely into place.

before you start

MATERIALS

DK-weight yarn (100% cotton; approx. 93 yds/85 m per 2 oz/50 g ball) in 3 colors:

A Red x 1 ball
B Pink x 1 ball
C Orange x 1 ball
D Fingering-weight yarn (70% super kid mohair, 30% silk; approx. 229 yds/210 m per 1 oz/25 g ball) x 1 ball (pink)
Yarn D is used doubled throughout
28 large glass beads

HOOK SIZE

G (4.5 mm)

GAUGE

Not important

FINISHED SIZE

3 x 70" (7 x 180 cm)

KEY TECHNIQUES

• Foundation chains, pages 19–20
• Single crochet, page 21
• Tassel fringe, page 52

ABBREVIATIONS

ch—chain
RS—right side
sc—single crochet
st(s)—stitch(es)

You can wear this scarf around the neck in the traditional way, or wrap it around your waist or hips instead—because it's so skinny, it won't add bulk!

quick-and-easy jewelry

THESE SMALL PROJECTS CAN REALLY SET OFF AN OUTFIT, FROM THE ELEGANT

AND SOPHISTICATED FILIGREE LACE CHOKER AND BEADED LADDER CHOKER TO

THE CONTEMPORARY CIRCULAR DISK NECKLACE. THE FLORAL CORSAGES CAN

BE PINNED ONTO ACCESSORIES AND GARMENTS ALIKE TO MAKE YOU STAND

OUT FROM THE CROWD. THE DELICATE BEADED BRACELET IS A BEAUTIFUL

EXAMPLE OF HOW TO CROCHET WITH MATERIALS OTHER THAN YARN.

Project 28: Rose corsages

These rose corsages are a delight to make as well as to look at. The smaller rose is worked in fine tweed-effect yarn. This speckled yarn is crocheted in tonal stripes to add a natural depth to the piece, which is then trimmed with a fine kid mohair/silk blend in a pretty picot stitch. The look of the corsage changes dramatically when worked in a bulky linen/viscose blend yarn with a mix of colors running through it, and edged with a cotton picot trim.

SMALL ROSE

Foundation chain: Using a size D (3 mm) hook and yarn A, ch 40.

Row 1 (RS): Ch 1, 1 sc into 2nd ch from hook, 1 sc into every ch to end.

Row 2: Ch 2, 2 dc into every sc to end (80 sts).

On the next row, the petal shape is created by using different lengths of stitches to give a curved appearance to the fabric edge. Change to yarn B.

before you start

MATERIALS

Small rose

Light-weight yarn (100% pure new wool; approx. 120 yds/110 m per 1 oz/25 g ball) in 2 colors:

A Purple x 1 ball

B Red x 1 ball

C Fingering-weight yarn (70% super kid mohair, 30% silk; approx. 229 yds/210 m per 1 oz/25 g ball) x 1 ball (pink)

Large rose

D Bulky-weight yarn (70% linen, 30% viscose; approx. 60 yds/ 55 m per 2 oz/50 g ball) x 1 ball (pink)

E Medium-weight yarn (100% cotton; approx. 125 yds/115 m per 2 oz/50 g ball) x 1 ball (purple)

1 pin clip for each corsage

HOOK SIZE

D (3 mm), J (6 mm)

GAUGE

Not important

FINISHED SIZE

Small rose: 3" (8 cm) diameter

Large rose: 5" (12 cm) diameter

KEY TECHNIQUES

- Foundation chains, pages 19–20
- Single crochet, page 21
- Double crochet, pages 22–3
- Half double crochet, page 23
- Treble crochet, page 24
- Seams, pages 33–4

ABBREVIATIONS

ch—chain

dc—double crochet

hdc—half double crochet

RS—right side

sc—single crochet

sl st—slip stitch

st(s)—stitch(es)

tr—treble crochet

Row 3: Ch 1, *1 sc, 1 hdc, 2 dc into next st, 3 tr into next st, 2 dc into next st, 1 hdc, 1 sc, 1 sl st, repeat from * to end (120 sts). Change to yarn C and work the picot chain trim as follows:

Row 4: *Ch 3, skip 1 st, sl st into next st, repeat from * to end.

Fasten off yarn.

LARGE ROSE

Using a size J (6 mm) hook and yarn D, work as instructed for the small rose but do not change colors when working the main body of the flower. Change to a size D (3 mm) hook and yarn E for the picot chain trim. Fasten off yarn.

FINISHING

For both roses, weave in any loose ends but do not block or press. To create the flower effect, coil the fabric around from the foundation chain. Sew the coiled shape together at the center, using yarn A for the small rose and yarn D for the large rose. Tease the petals into position and attach a pin clip to the back.

These rose corsages clearly demonstrate the different results that you can achieve by using different yarns. The smaller rose worked in finer yarns has a delicate appeal, while the bulkier yarns of the large rose produce a stunning show stopper.

Project 29: Chrysanthemum corsage

This fantastic corsage is worked in three separate pieces, using two different weights of yarn and different lengths of flower petals. When layered together, the resulting corsage has depth and a sense of movement. The center is filled with a wooden bead surrounded by hand-embroidered French knots.

before you start

MATERIALS

A Aran-weight yarn (70% silk, 30% cotton; approx. 118 yds/108 m per 2 oz/50 g ball) x 1 ball (green)
B DK-weight yarn (100% cotton; approx. 95 yds/87 m 2 oz/50 g ball) x 1 ball (ecru)
1 round wooden bead
Embroidery thread
1 pin clip

HOOK SIZE

H (5 mm), F (4 mm)

GAUGE

Not important

FINISHED SIZE

4¼" (11 cm) diameter

KEY TECHNIQUES

• Foundation chains, pages 19–20
• Single crochet, page 21
• Working in rounds, page 25

ABBREVIATIONS

ch—chain
RS—right side
sc—single crochet
sl st—slip stitch
st(s)—stitch(es)

FIRST FLOWER

Foundation ring: Using a size H (5 mm) hook and yarn A, ch 6 and join with sl st to form a ring.

Round 1 (RS): Ch 2, 14 sc into center of ring, sl st into 2nd ch of ch 2.

Round 2: Ch 15, sl st into first sc (this makes one petal), *1 sc into next sc, ch 15, sl st into sc just worked, repeat from * until 15 petal loops worked, sl st into first sc.
Fasten off yarn.

SECOND FLOWER

Work as instructed for the first flower but use a size F (4 mm) hook and yarn B.

THIRD FLOWER

Foundation ring: Using a size F (4 mm) hook and yarn B, ch 6 and join with sl st to form a ring.

Round 1 (RS): Ch 2, 11 sc into center of ring, sl st into 2nd ch of ch 2.

Round 2: Ch 10, sl st into first sc, *1 sc into next sc, ch 10, sl st into sc just worked, repeat from * until 12 petal loops worked, sl st in to first sc.
Fasten off yarn.

FINISHING

Weave in any loose ends. Layer the flowers together with the largest at the bottom and the smallest on top. Sew together at their centers using yarn B, then sew a wooden bead to the center of the corsage. Work French knots around the bead, then attach a pin clip to the back.

New skills/french knots

French knots work really well on crochet, adding a three-dimensional aspect to a flat fabric. They look especially good as flower centers.

1 Bring the needle through the work from back to front. Wrap the yarn around the needle once or twice.

2 Pull the yarn taut so that the wraps are tight against the needle, then take the needle through to the back of the work close to where the yarn first came through.

Corsages are not just for evening wear. This pretty floral brooch is worked in natural shades and embellished with a wooden bead to make it perfect for dressing up a garment, bag, or other accessory.

Project 30: Delicate beaded bracelet

This delicate beaded bracelet can easily be crocheted in a single evening. Worked in a fine yet durable gold wire and threaded with a mixture of beads in different colors and sizes, the single crochet stitch design looks far more complicated that it really is.

before you start

MATERIALS
1 reel of 0.2 mm gold jewelry wire
Approx. 10 medium lime green beads
Approx. 12 small lime green beads
Approx. 15 small dark green beads
Approx. 15 small metallic gray beads
1 gold clasp and ring

HOOK SIZE
6 steel (1.75 mm)

GAUGE
Not important

FINISHED SIZE
7½" (19 cm) long, excluding clasp

KEY TECHNIQUES
• Foundation chains, pages 19–20
• Single crochet, page 21
• Incorporating beads, page 88

ABBREVIATIONS
bsc—beaded single crochet
ch—chain
RS—right side
sc—single crochet

CROCHETING THE BRACELET
Thread 3–4 small beads and then 1 large bead onto the wire, alternating the colors to give a random effect. Remember that the first bead you thread on will be the last bead worked.
Foundation chain: Using a size 6 (1.75 mm) steel hook and jewelry wire, ch 36.
Row 1 (RS): Ch 1, 2 sc, 1 bsc, *1 sc, 1 bsc, repeat from * 15 times, 3 sc.
Row 2: Ch 1, 1 sc into every sc and bsc to end.
Fine jewelry wire can be difficult to work with if you are not used to it, but don't worry if you do not work each stitch in the exact place because this will just add to the random feel of the piece. All that is important is that you have the correct number of stitches.

Row 3: Repeat row 1.
Row 4: Repeat row 2.
Row 5: Repeat row 1.
Fasten off wire.

FINISHING
Using wire, attach a clasp and the accompanying ring to opposite ends of the bracelet.

TIP: KEEPING COUNT
When crocheting with such fine wire, keep a careful count of stitches and rows as you go because they are difficult to count after they have been worked.

The wire and clasp can either be real gold or simply gold colored. There are many different colors of jewelry wire available, so choose one to complement the beads you want to use.

Project 31: Circular disk necklace

Personalized jewelry is very fashionable at the moment, especially necklaces. This eye-catching piece is extremely easy to make, and will add that hip touch to any outfit. The necklace is made up of a series of circular disks, each one worked in brightly colored rings of compact single crochet stitch to create a bold and beautiful look.

LARGE DISK (MAKE 2)

Foundation ring: Following the color sequences indicated below and using a size D (3 mm) hook, ch 5 and join with sl st to form a ring.

Round 1 (RS): Ch 1, 9 sc into center of ring, sl st into first ch of round.

Round 2: Ch 1, 2 sc into every sc, sl st into first sc (18 sts).

Round 3: Ch 1, 1 sc into every sc, sl st into first sc.

Round 4: Ch 1, 1 sc, *2 sc into next sc, 1 sc, repeat from * to end, sl st into first sc. Fasten off yarn.

FIRST DISK COLORS
Ring: Yarn E.
Rounds 1–2: Yarn E.
Round 3: Yarn A.
Round 4: Yarn D.

SECOND DISK COLORS
Ring: Yarn D.
Rounds 1–3: Yarn D.
Round 4: Yarn F.

SMALL DISK (MAKE 5)

Work as instructed for the large disk, but fasten off the yarn after round 3. Follow the color sequences indicated below.

FIRST DISK COLORS
Ring: Yarn C.
Rounds 1–2: Yarn C.
Round 3: Yarn F.

SECOND DISK COLORS
Ring: Yarn B.
Rounds 1–2: Yarn B.
Round 3: Yarn D.

THIRD DISK COLORS
Ring: Yarn C.
Rounds 1–2: Yarn C.
Round 3: Yarn A.

FOURTH DISK COLORS
Ring: Yarn B.
Round 1: Yarn B.
Round 2: Yarn C.
Round 3: Yarn E.

FIFTH DISK COLORS
Ring: Yarn A.
Round 1: Yarn A.
Round 2: Yarn G.
Round 3: Yarn F.

FINISHING

Weave in any loose ends. Using a size D (3 mm) hook and yarn G, join the disks and create the ties as follows: leaving a long tail, ch 60, 2 sc into top of small disk, ch 5, 2 sc into top of small disk, ch 5, 2 sc into top of large disk, ch 5, 2 sc into top of small disk, ch 5, 2 sc into top of large disk, ch 5, 2 sc into top of small disk, ch 5, 2 sc into top of small disk, ch 60. Fasten off yarn, leaving a long tail.

before you start

MATERIALS
Scraps of medium-weight yarn (100% cotton; approx. 125 yds/ 115 m per 2 oz/50 g ball) in 6 colors:
A Purple
B Yellow
C Lilac
D Lime
E Dark green
F Blue
G Scraps of gold light-weight yarn (80% viscose, 20% polyester; approx. 104 yds/95 m per 1 oz/25 g ball)

HOOK SIZE
D (3 mm)

GAUGE
Not important

FINISHED SIZE
Large disk: 1¾" (4.5 cm) diameter
Small disk: 1¼" (3 cm) diameter

KEY TECHNIQUES
• Foundation chains, pages 19–20
• Single crochet, page 21
• Working in rounds, page 25

ABBREVIATIONS
ch—chain
RS—right side
sc—single crochet
sl st—slip stitch
st(s)—stitch(es)

It is easy to adapt
this necklace to
make a personal
statement: alter
the colors, the
number of rounds,
or the length of
the chain. You
could also make a
matching bracelet.

Project 32: Filigree lace choker

This sparkling evening choker looks fantastic but, worked over just two rows, it is actually very simple to make. The use of a light-weight gold lurex yarn to work the filigree lace motifs gives the choker its glamorous appearance.

before you start

MATERIALS
Light-weight yarn (80% viscose, 20% polyester; approx. 104 yds/95 m per 1 oz/25 g ball) x 1 ball (gold) 1 medium-sized button

HOOK SIZE
D (3 mm)

GAUGE
Exact gauge is not important as long as the choker fits snugly around the neck, but is not too tight or too loose; the pattern is repeated over 7 sts + 1, so try working the pattern over 3 repeats to see whether you need to make the foundation chain longer or shorter than instructed

FINISHED SIZE
12" (30 cm) long unstretched

KEY TECHNIQUES
• Foundation chains, pages 19–20
• Single crochet, page 21
• Double crochet, pages 22–3
• Treble crochet, page 24

ABBREVIATIONS
ch—chain
dc—double crochet
RS—right side
sc—single crochet
sl st—slip stitch
st(s)—stitch(es)
tr—treble crochet

CROCHETING THE CHOKER
Foundation chain: Using a size D (3 mm) hook, ch 76.
Row 1 (RS): Ch 1, 1 sc into 2nd ch from hook, 1 sc into next ch 5, *turn, ch 7, skip 5 sc, 1 sc into next sc, turn, (6 sc, ch 5, 6 sc) into ch 7 space, 1 sc into next foundation ch 7, repeat from *, ending with 1 sc into last foundation ch.
Row 2: Ch 4, skip first sc, *skip next 6 sc, (1 dc, ch 3, 1 sl st into first of these ch 3) 4 times into ch 5 space, 1 dc into same ch 5 space, skip 6 sc, 1 tr into next sc, repeat from * to end, working last tr into ch 1.
Fasten off yarn.

FINISHING
Sew a button to one end of the choker. Make a button loop at the opposite end by working a small chain and joining the other end of the chain to the choker with a slip stitch to form a loop.

This Edwardian-style golden choker, with its intricate lace motifs, is a classic design that has a timeless appeal. The light-weight metallic yarn beautifully accentuates the filigree lace work.

Project 33: Beaded ladder choker

Using the most basic crochet stitches, this beautiful beaded choker can easily be made in a few hours. Worked in a bright medium-weight cotton yarn and embellished with pretty glass beads, the only difficult thing will be deciding which colors to choose to complement your wardrobe.

before you start

MATERIALS

Medium-weight yarn (100% cotton; approx. 125 yds/115 m per 2 oz/50 g ball) x 1 ball (green)
200 small glass beads
Press-stud fastener or Velcro spot

HOOK SIZE

F (4 mm)

GAUGE

4 repeats of ladder pattern = 4" (10 cm) long

FINISHED SIZE

1 x 13" (2.5 x 33 cm)

KEY TECHNIQUES

• Foundation chains, pages 19–20
• Single crochet, page 21
• Extended single crochet, page 22
• Incorporating beads, page 88
• Beaded chain, page 118

ABBREVIATIONS

bch—beaded chain
bsc—beaded single crochet
ch—chain
exsc—extended single crochet
RS—right side
sc—single crochet
st(s)—stitch(es)

CROCHETING THE CHOKER

Thread all the beads onto the yarn.
Foundation chain: Using a size F (4 mm) hook, 78 bch.
Row 1 (RS): Ch 6, 1 sc into 13th bch from hook, *ch 5, skip 5 bch, 1 bsc, repeat from *, ending ch 5, skip ch 5, 1 exsc into last ch.
Row 2: Ch 7, skip first exsc, *skip ch 5, 1 bsc into next bsc, ch 5, repeat from * ending ch 5, skip ch 5, 1 exsc into next ch.
Row 3: Repeat row 2.
Row 4: 7 bch, skip first exsc, *skip ch 5, 1 bsc into next bsc, 5 bch, repeat from * ending 5 bsc, skip ch 5, 1 exsc into last ch.

FINISHING

Weave in any loose ends, then block and press to the correct size. Work 1 sc into one end of the choker to create a small extension, then fasten off yarn. Sew a press stud or Velcro spot to the ends of the choker.

TIP: ADJUSTING THE LENGTH

The ladder stitch used in this pattern is worked over a multiple of 6 sts + 1 (add 6 for foundation chain). To shorten or lengthen the choker, simply adjust the total number of stitches worked by multiples of 7.

New skills/beaded chain

Incorporating beads into the foundation chain is very easy to do.

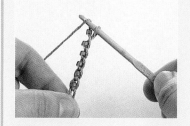

1 Make a slip knot in the usual way, then bring a bead up to the top of the yarn, place the bead under the hook, and wrap the yarn over the hook.

2 Pull the yarn through the loop, leaving the bead at the front of the work, lying on the chain. Continue in this way for each beaded chain stitch required in the pattern.

The brightly colored beads frame each section of the ladder stitch crochet work to give the choker depth and structure. Refer to the tip on adjusting the length of the choker if you would like to make a matching bracelet.

Yarn directory

Below is a list of the specific yarns used to make the projects. However, if you cannot find any of these yarns or simply wish to make a project in a different yarn, use the information supplied at the beginning of each project, where you will find the quantity, weight, and fiber content of the yarns. Additional advice on substituting yarns can be found on page 14.

BAGS & PURSES

Project 1: Slash-handled bag
Yarn: Rowan Yorkshire Tweed DK; colors & codes: A = Cheer 343, B = Skip 347, C = Scarlet 344, D = Frolic 350, E = Frog 349, F = Goose 352.

Project 2: Acid-bright zigzag bag
Yarn: Rowan Handknit Cotton; colors & codes: A = Decadent 314, B = Seafarer 318, C = Slick 313, D = Flame 254, E = Mango Fool 319.

Project 3: Bulb bag
Yarn: Rowan Handknit Cotton; color & code: Decadent 314.

Project 4: Big shopping bag
Yarn A: Rowan Big Wool; color & code: Tricky 030. Yarn B: Rowan Biggy Print; color & code: Tickle 237.

Project 5: Evening purses
Yarn: Rowan Lurex Shimmer; color & code: A = Pewter 333, B = Minty 337.

THROWS & PILLOWS

Project 6: Softly textured throw
Yarn A: Rowan Kid Classic; color & code: Wild 816. Yarn B: Rowan Biggy Print; color & code: Sheep 258.

Project 7: Softly textured pillow
Yarn A: Rowan Kid Classic; color & code: Bear 817. Yarn B: Rowan Biggy Print; color & code: Cookie 243.

Project 8: Ruffle throw
Yarn: Rowan Kid Classic; color & code: Feather 828.

Project 9: Ruffle pillow
Yarn: Rowan Kid Classic; color & code: Glacier 822.

Project 10: Funky floor pillow
Yarn: Rowan Plaid; colors & codes: A = Washed Pebbles 165, B = Spicy 154, C = Creeper 155, D = Bramble 157, E = Nuzzle 158, F = Hearty 156, G = Stormy Night 168.

HATS, MITTENS & BELTS

Project 11: Pointed pixie hat
Yarn: Rowan Plaid; color & code: Hearty 156.

Project 12: Striped beanie
Yarn: Rowan Chunky Print; color & code: A = Woolly 071, B = Rage 079.

Project 13: Striped mittens
Yarn: Rowan Chunky Print; color & code: A = Woolly 071, B = Rage 079.

Project 14: Mock cable tie belt
Yarn: Rowan Denim; color & code: Ecru 324.

Project 15: Denim square tie belt
Yarn: Rowan Denim; colors & codes: A = Ecru 324, B = Nashville 225, C = Tennessee 231.

WRAPS & GARMENTS

Project 16: Lacy cape
Yarn: Rowan Plaid; color & code: Washed Pebbles 165.

Project 17: Picot-mesh wrap
Yarn A: Rowan Big wool; color & code: White Hot 001. Yarn B: Rowan Chunky Print; color & code: Woolly 071.

Project 18: Lace evening wrap
Yarn: Jaeger Silk 4ply; color & code: Brilliant 144.

Project 19: Open-mesh shrug
Yarn: Rowan Plaid; color & code: Creeper 155.

Project 20: Beaded wrap
Yarn: Rowan Kidsilk Haze; color & code: Pearl 590.

Project 21: Striped poncho
Yarns A & B: Rowan Kid Classic; color & code: A = Cherry Red 847, B = Juicy 827. Yarn C: Rowan Biggy Print; color & code: Tickle 237.

SCARVES

Project 22: Bobbles on a string
Yarn A: Rowan Biggy Print; color & code: Savage 256. Yarn B: Rowan Yorkshire Tweed DK; color & code: Revel 342. Yarn C: Rowan Yorkshire Tweed Aran; color & code: Hero 411. Yarn D: Rowan Yorkshire Tweed Chunky; color & code: Olive Oil 557.

Project 23: Sequinned scarf
Yarn: Rowan Kidsilk Haze; color & code: Meadow 581.

Project 24: Pompon-trimmed scarf
Yarn: Rowan Chunky print; color & code: Shriek 081.

Project 25: Chevron-striped scarf
Yarns A–C: Rowan Cotton Glace; colors & codes: A = Shoot 814, B = Tickle 811, C = Oyster 730. Yarn D: Rowan Lurex Shimmer; color & code: Minty 337.

Project 26: Cozy felted scarf
Yarns A & B: Rowan Yorkshire Tweed Aran; colors & codes: A = Tusk 417, B = Darkside 414. Yarn C: Rowan Yorkshire Tweed DK; color & code: Scarlet 344. Yarn D: Rowan Kidsilk Haze; color & code: Blushes 583.

Project 27: Skinny beaded scarf
Yarns A–C: Rowan Handknit Cotton; colors & codes: A = Rosso 215, B = Slick 313, C = Mango Fool 319. Yarn D: Rowan Lurex Shimmer; color & code: Bedazzled 338.

JEWELRY

Project 28: Rose corsages
Yarns A & B: Rowan Yorkshire Tweed 4ply; color & code: A = Foxy 275, B = Brilliant 274. Yarn C: Rowan Kidsilk Haze; color & code: Candy Girl 606. Yarn D: Rowan Linen Print; color & code: Crush 347. Yarn E: Rowan Cotton Glace; color & code: Excite 815.

Project 29: Chrysanthemum corsage
Yarn A: Rowan Summer Tweed; color & code: Sprig 527. Yarn B: Rowan Handknit Cotton; color & code: Ecru 251.

Project 31: Circular disk necklace
Yarns A–F: Rowan Cotton Glace; colors & codes: A = Excite 815, B = Zeal 813, C = Tickle 811, D = Shoot 814, E = Ivy 812, F = Splendour 810. Yarn G: Rowan Lurex Shimmer; color & code: Antique White Gold 332.

Project 32: Filigree lace choker
Yarn: Rowan Lurex Shimmer; color & code: Antique White Gold 332.

Project 33: Beaded ladder choker
Yarn: Rowan Cotton Glace; color & code: Shoot 814.

Resources

MIDWEST

Illinois
Arcadia Knitting
Chicago, IL 60640
773-293-1211

Sunflower Samplings
Crystal Lake, IL 60014
815-455-2919

Three Bags Full
Northbrook, IL 60062
847-291-9933

Indiana
Mass. Ave. Knit Shop
Indianapolis, IN 46203
317-638-1833

River Knits
Lafayette, IN 47901
765-742-5648

Sheep St. Fibers, Inc.
Morgantown, IN 46160
812-597-5648

Iowa
Creative Corner
W. Des Moines, IA 50265
515-255-7262

The Knitting Shop
Iowa City, IA 52240
319-337-4920

Three Oaks Knits
Cedar Falls, IA 50613
319-266-6221

Kansas
Laura May's Cottage
Lindsborg, KS 67456
785-227-3948

Wildflower Yarns and Knitwear
Manhattan, KS 66502
785-537-1826
www.wildflowerknits.com
wldflwr@kansas.net

Yarn Barn
Lawrence, KS 66044
785-842-4333

Michigan
City Knits
Detroit, MI 48202
313-872-9665

Knit a Round Yarn Shop
Ann Arbor, MI 48105
734-998-3771

The Wool & the Floss
Grosse Point, MI 48230
313-882-9110

Minnesota
Linden Hills Yarns
Minneapolis, MN 55410
612-929-1255

Three Kitten Yarn Shoppe
St Paul, MN 55118
651-457-4969

Yarnworks
Grand Rapids, MN 55744
218-327-1898

Missouri
Chris' Needlecraft Supplies
Chesterfield, MO 63017
314-205-8766

Hearthstone Knits
St. Louis, MO 63123
314-849-9276

Simply Fibers Ltd.
Springfield, MO 65807
417-881-Yarn

Nebraska
Personal Threads
Omaha, NE 68114
402-391-7733

Plum Nelly
Hastings, NE 68901
402-462-2490

String of Purls
Omaha, NE 68114
402-393-5648

North Dakota
Bandanas and Bows
Medora, ND 58645
701-623-4347

Ohio
The Knitting Room
Cleveland, OH 44122
216-464-8450

Peach Mountain Studio
Cincinnati, OH 45243
513-271-3191

Wolfe Fiber Arts, Inc.
Columbus, OH 43212
614-487-9980

South Dakota
Ben Franklin Crafts
Mitchell, SD 57301
605-996-5464

Wisconsin
Alphabet Soup
Madison, WI 53705
608-238-1329

Barbara's Yarn Garden
Racine, WI 53402
262-632-7725

Monterey Yarn
Green Bay, WI 54311
920-884-5258

NORTHEAST

Connecticut
Mystic River Yarns
Mystic, CT 06355
860-536-4305

Yarns Down Under
Deep River, CT 06417
860-526-9986
www.yarnsdownunder.com

Yarns with a Twist
Chaplin, CT 06235
860-455-9986
yarnswithatwist@yahoo.com

Delaware
Knit2purl2
Newark, Delaware 19711
302-737-4917
www.knit2purl2.com
jody@knit2purl2.com

Maine
Cityside Yarn Co.
Bangor, ME 04401
207-990-1455

Knitwit Yarn Shop and Cafe
Portland, ME 04101
207-774-6444

Water Street Yarns
Hallowell, ME 04347
207-622-5500

Massachusetts
Sheep to Shore
Nantucket, MA 02554
508-228-0038

Wild and Woolly Studio
Lexington, MA 02420
781-861-7717 wwoolly@aol.com

Windsor Button
Boston, MA 02111
617-482-4969
orders@Windsorbutton.com

New Jersey
The Knitting Room
Medford, NJ 08055
609-654-9003

The Knitting Store
Cherry Hill, NJ 08003
856-751-7750
theknittingstore@comcast.net

Wooly Monmouth
Red Bank, NJ 07701
732-224-YARN
www.woolymonmouth.com

New Hampshire
Charlotte's Web
Exeter, NH 03833
603-778-1417

The Elegant Ewe
Concord, NH 03301
603-226-0066
www.elegantewe.com

Spinning Yarns
Dover, NH 03820
603-740-6476

Westminster Fibers
4 Townsend West, Unit 8
Nashua, NH 03063

New York
Downtown Yarns
New York, NY 10009
212-995-5991

Knit 'n Purl
Rochester, NY 14618
585-442-7420

Knitting Fever, Inc.
35 Debevoise Avenue
Roosevelt, NY 11575
www.knittingfever.com

Rock City Yarn
Woodstock, NY 12498
845-679-9600

Pennsylvania
Knitter's Dream
Harrisburg, PA 17112
717-599-7665
www.knittersdream.com
Knittersdream@aol.com

Pittsburgh Knit and Bead
Pittsburgh, PA 15217
412-421-7522

Unique Kolours, LLC
28 N. Bacton Hill Road
Malvern, PA 19355
800-252-3934
www.uniquekolours.com
uniquekolo@aol.com

Yarn Basket
Chambersburg, PA 17201
717-263-3236

Rhode Island
Craft Corner
Woonsocket, RI 02895
401-762-3233

Yarn Outlet
Pawtucket, RI 02860
401-722-5600

Vermont
Naked Sheep
Bennington, VT 05201
802-440-9653

Pine Ledge Fiber Studio
Fairfax, VT 05454
802-849-9731

River Muse Yarn
Johnson, VT 05656
802-635-9851
rivermuse@msn.com

PACIFIC

Alaska
Changing Threads
326 Third Ave
Skagway, AK 99840
907-983-3700
www.changingthreads.com

Knitting Frenzy
Anchorage, AK 99503
907-563-2717

A Weaver's Yarn
Fairbanks, AK 99708
907-322-5050

California
Ancient Pathways
Fresno, CA 93728
559-264-1874

Black Sheep Knitting
Los Angeles, CA 90028
323-464-2253

The Grove at Juniper and 30th
San Diego, CA 92104
619-284-7684

Knitting Room
San Jose, CA 95124
408-264-7229

Knitting Basket
Oakland, CA 94611
510-339-6295
info@theknittingbasket.com

The Knitty Gritty
Anaheim, CA 92805
714-778-2340
www.theknittygritty.com

Paper Habit
Modesto, CA 95350
209-567-0605

Stash
Berkeley, CA 94707
510-558-9276
contact@stashyarn.com

Straw Into Gold
160 23rd Street
Richmond, CA 94804
www.crystalpalaceyarns.com
cpy@straw.com

The Swift Stitch
Santa Cruz, CA 95060
831-427-9276

Trendsetter Yarns
16745 Saticoy Street, Suite 101
Van Nuys, CA 91406
818-780-5497
www.trendsetteryarns.com
info@trendsetteryarns.com

Unicorn Books and Crafts, Inc.
1338 Ross Street
Petaluma, CA 94954
800-BUY-YARN
www.unicornbooks.com

Urban Knitting Studio
San Francisco, CA 94102
415-552-5333
helen@urbanknitting.com

Wildfiber
Santa Monica, CA 90404
310-458-2748

The Yarn Boutique
Lafayette, CA 94549
925-283-7377
www.yarnboutique.us
yarnboutique@sbcglobal.net

Hawaii
Aloha Yarn
Kaneohe, HI 96744
808-234-5865

Big Island Bernina
Hilo, HI 96720
808-929-0034

Isle Knit
Honolulu, HI 96813
808-533-0853

Oregon
Artistic Needles
Salem, OR 97301
503-589-1502

The Cozy Ewe
Oregon City, OR 97045
503-723-5255

Knit Shop, Inc.
Eugene, OR 97405
541-434-0430

Northwest Wools
Portland, OR 97219
503-244-5024

Yarn Expressions
Huntsville, AL 35802-2274
256-881-0260

Arkansas
Designing Yarns
Jonesboro, AR 72401
870-972-9537

Hand Held Knitting Gallery
Fayetteville, AR 72701
479-582-2910

Yarn Mart
Little Rock, AR 72207
501-666-6505

Florida
Elegant Stitches
Miami, FL 33176
305-232-4005

Knit 'n Knibble
Tampa, FL 33629
813-254-5648

Yarn Works
Gainesville, FL 32609
352-337-9965

Georgia
In Stitches
Augusta, GA 30907
706-868-9276

The Knitting Emporium
Kennesaw, GA 30144
770-421-1919

Needle Nook
Atlanta, GA 30329-3449
404-325-0068

Kentucky
Carma Needlecraft, Inc.
Louisville, KY 40222
502-425-4170

The Stitche Niche, Inc.
Lexington, KY 40503
859-277-2604

Stone's Throw Artisans
Georgetown, KY 40324
502-867-5897

Louisiana
The Yarn Nook
Crowley, LA 70526
337-783-5565
www.yarnnook.com

Maryland
Keep Me in Stitches!
Frederick, MD 21701
240-379-7740

Woolstock
Glyndon, MD 21071
410-517-1020

Woolworks
Baltimore, MD 21209
410-337-9030

Mississippi
Knit Wits
Jackson, MS 39211
601-957-9098

North Carolina
Knit One Smock Too
Winston Salem, NC 27104
336-765-9099

The Sewing Bird
Charlotte, NC 28209
704-676-0076

This and That
Greensboro, NC 27408
336-275-0044

Oklahoma
Gourmet Yarn Co.
Oklahoma City, OK 73120
405-286-3737

Naturally Needlepoint
Tulsa, OK 74105
918-747-8838

Sealed with a Kiss, Inc.
Guthrie, OK 73044
405-282-8649

South Carolina
Island Knits
The Island Shops
Pawleys Island, SC 29585
843-235-0110

Washington
Acorn Street Yarn Shop
Seattle, WA 98105
206-525-1726

Amanda's Art Yarns
Poulsbo, WA 98370
360-779-3666

Hank & Bolt Co.
Bellingham, WA 98225
360-733-7836

King Cole and Cascade Yarns
PO Box 58168
Tukwila, WA 98188
www.cascadeyarns.com

Lamb's Ear
Tacoma, WA 98408
253-472-7695
rockfarm@gte.net
www.lambsearfarm.com

SOUTH

Alabama
Heidi's Yarnhaus
Mobile, AL 36609
251-342-0088
www.yarnhaus.com
yarnhaus@aol.com

Memory Hagler Knitting
Birmingham, AL 35216
205-822-7875

Knit
Charleston, SC 29403
843-937-8500

Tennessee
Angel Hair Yarn Co.
Nashville, TN 37215
615-269-8833

Genuine Purl
Chattanooga, TN 37405
423-267-7335

The Yarn Studio
Memphis, TN 38104
901-276-5442

Texas
Desert Designs Knitz
Dallas, TX 75254
972-392-9276

Hill Country Weavers
Austin, TX 78704
512-707-7396

Nimble Fingers
Houston, TX 77024
713-722-7244

Virginia
Knitting Basket
Richmond, VA 23226
804-282-2909
www.theknittingbasket.biz

Knitting Sisters
Williamsburg, VA 23185
757-258-5005
www.knittingsisters.com
info@knittingsisters.com

Knitwits
Virginia Beach, VA 23464
757-495-6600

Washington, DC
Stitch DC, Inc.
Washington, DC 20003
202-487-4337

West Virginia
Kanawha City Yarn Co.
Charleston, WV 25304
304-926-8589

WEST

Arizona
A Back Door Bead
and Yarn Co.
Tucson, AZ 85712
520-745-9080
nancy@bdbeads.com

Knitting in Scottsdale
Scottsdale, AZ 85254
480-951-9942

Unravel Yarns
Flagstaff, AZ 86001
928-556-9276
www.unravelshop.com

Colorado
A Knitted Peace
Littleton, CO 80120
303-730-0366

Showers of Flowers
6900 West Colfax Avenue
Lakewood, CO 80215
http://showersofflowers.com

Strawberry Tree
Denver, CO 80222
303-759-4244

Idaho
Drop a Stitch
Boise, ID 83702
208-331-3767

Isabell's Needlepoint
Ketchum, ID 83340
208-725-0408

Sheep to Shawl
Twin Falls, ID 83301
208-735-8425

Montana
Knit 'n Needle
Whitefish, MT 59937
406-862-6390

Pam's Knit 'n Stitch
Great Falls, MT 59401
406-761-4652

Stix
Bozeman, MT 59715
406-556-5786
www.stix.com

Nevada
Deluxe Yarns etc.
Reno, NV 89509
775-322-1244

Gail Knits
Las Vegas, NV 89117
702-838-7713

Wooly Wonders
Las Vegas, NV 89121
702-547-1661

New Mexico
Three Stitchers
Clovis, NM 88101
505-762-0295

Village Wools
Albuquerque, NM 87110
505-883-2919

The Yarn Shop
Taos, NM 87571
505-758-9341

Utah
Heindselman's
Provo, UT 84601
801-373-5193

Judy's Novelty Wool
Centerville, UT 84014
801-298-1356

Soul Spun
Salt Lake City, UT 84109
801-746-5094

Wyoming
In Sheep's Clothing
Laramie, WY 82070
307-755-9276

Knit on Purl
Jackson, WY 83001
307-733-5648

Over the Moon
Sheridan, WY 82801
307-673-5991

WEB RESOURCES

The Craft Yarn Council
www.craftyarncouncil.com

The Crochet Guild of America
www.crochet.org

SELECTED SUPPLIERS
www.buy-mail.co.uk
www.coatscrafts.co.uk
www.colourway.co.uk
www.coolwoolz.co.uk
www.designeryarns.uk.com
www.diamondyarns.com
www.ethknits.co.uk
www.e-yarn.com
www.handworksgallery.com
www.hantex.co.uk
www.hook-n-needle.com
www.kangaroo.uk.com
www.karpstyles.ca
www.kgctrading.com
www.knitrowan.com (features worldwide
   list of stockists of Rowan yarns)
www.knittersdream.com/yarn
www.knittingfever.com
www.knitwellwools.co.uk
www.lacis.com
www.maggiescrochet.com
www.mcadirect.com
www.patternworks.com
www.patonsyarns.com
www.personalthreads.com
www.sakonnetpurls.com
www.shetland-wool-brokers-zetnet.co.uk
www.sirdar.co.uk
www.spiningayarn.com
www.theknittinggarden.com
www.upcountry.co.uk
www.yarncompany.com
www.yarnexpressions.com
www.yarnmarket.com

Glossary

Ball band The paper strip around a ball of yarn giving information about weight, shade number, dye lot number, fiber content, and care instructions. A ball band may also contain other details including yardage and suggested gauge.

Blocking Setting a piece of crochet by stretching and pinning it out on a flat surface before steaming or treating with cold water.

Border A deep, decorative strip of crochet, usually worked with one straight and one shaped edge, that is used for trimming pieces of crochet or fabric.

Braid A narrow, decorative strip of crochet similar in appearance to a purchased furnishing braid.

Chain space Space formed by working strands of chain stitches between other stitches. Also known as chain loops or chain arches.

Decrease To reduce the number of working stitches.

Dye lot The batch of dye used for a specific ball of yarn. Shades can vary between batches, so use yarn from the same dye lot to make an item.

Edge finish A decorative crochet edging worked directly into the edge of a piece of crochet.

Edging A narrow strip of crochet, usually with one straight and one shaped edge, used for trimming pieces of crochet or fabric.

Fiber Naturally occurring or manmade substances spun together to make yarn.

Filet crochet A type of patterned crochet where the pattern elements are worked solidly and set against a regularly worked mesh background. Filet crochet is usually worked from a graphic chart rather than written instructions.

Foundation chain A length of chain stitches that forms the base row for a piece of crochet.

Foundation row In a stitch pattern, the first row worked after the foundation chain that is not repeated as part of the pattern.

Gauge The looseness or tightness of a crochet fabric expressed as a specific number of rows and stitches in a given area, usually 4" (10 cm) square.

Heading Extra rows of plain crochet worked on the long straight edge of an edging or border to add strength and durability.

Increase To make the number of working stitches larger.

Motif A shaped piece of crochet, often worked in rounds. Several motifs can be joined together rather like fabric patchwork to make a larger piece. Also known as a medallion.

Pattern A set of instructions showing how to make a garment or other crochet item.

Pattern repeat The specific number of rows or rounds that are needed to complete one stitch pattern.

Picot A decorative chain space, often closed into a ring with a slip stitch. The number of chains in a picot can vary.

Ply A single strand of yarn. Different numbers of plies are twisted together to make different yarns.

Right side The front of crochet fabric. This side is usually visible on a finished item.

Round A row of crochet worked in the round. Rounds are usually worked without turning so that the right side is always facing the worker and the end of one round is joined to the beginning of the same round.

Row A line of stitches worked from side to side of a flat piece of crochet.

Seam The join made where two pieces of crochet are stitched or crocheted together.

Sewing needle A needle with a sharp point used for applying a crochet braid, edging, or border to a piece of fabric.

Starting chain A specific number of chain stitches worked at the beginning of a round to bring the hook up to the correct height for the next stitch that is being worked.

Stitch pattern A sequence or combination of crochet stitches that is repeated over and over again to create a piece of crochet fabric.

Tapestry needle A large, blunt-ended embroidery needle used for sewing pieces of crochet together.

Turning chain A specific number of chain stitches worked at the beginning of a row to bring the hook up to the correct height for the next stitch that is being worked.

Wrong side The reverse side of crochet fabric. This side is not usually visible on a finished item.

AMERICAN/ENGLISH TERMINOLOGY

The patterns in this book use American terminology. Patterns published using English terminology can be very confusing because some English terms differ from the American system, as shown below:

American	English
single crochet (sc)	double crochet (dc)
extended single crochet (exsc)	extended double crochet (exdc)
half double crochet (hdc)	half treble crochet (htr)
double crochet (dc)	treble crochet (tr)
treble crochet (tr)	double treble crochet (dtr)
double treble crochet (dtr)	triple treble crochet (trtr or ttr)

Index

Credits

Quarto would like to thank and acknowledge Writtle College, Chelmsford, Essex CM1 3RR, England, +44 (0)1245 424 200, for allowing us to use their grounds for photography. Thanks also to the models—Kryssy Moss, Lynne Shillitto, and Tracey Lushington—and hair and make-up stylist Jackie Jones.

All photographs and illustrations are the copyright of Quarto Publishing plc.

Author's acknowledgments
Many thanks to Kate Buller and the rest of the team at Rowan for their help and support, and for the use of the lovely Rowan yarns. Thanks also to my Mum (Sandra Youngson) and Irene Jackson for helping me to create the projects, and to all my friends and loved ones for putting up with me.